JOHN DEERE
Photographic History

JOHN DEERE
Photographic History

Robert N. Pripps

Motorbooks International
Publishers & Wholesalers ®

First published in 1995 by Motorbooks International Publishers & Wholesalers, PO Box 2, 729 Prospect Avenue, Osceola, WI 54020 USA

Motorbooks International books are also available at discounts in bulk quantity for industrial or sales-promotional use. For details write to Special Sales Manager at the Publisher's address

Library of Congress Cataloging-in-Publication Data

Pripps, Robert N.
    John Deere photographic history/Robert Pripps.
        p. cm.
    Includes bibliographical references (p.) and index.
    ISBN 0-7603-0058-5 (pbk.)
    1. John Deere tractors—History. 2. John Deere tractors—Pictorial works. 3. Deere & Company—History. 4. Deere & Company—Pictorial works. 5. Agricultural machinery industry—United States—Pictorial works. I. Title.
TL233.5.P763   1995
629.225—dc20   95-36495

On the front cover: Don Wolf owns this 1930 Model GP, serial number 219083. *Andrew Morland*

On the back cover: A 1937 Model A tractor with a A492 mounted cultivator. *Deere Archives*; This 1938 "Styled" Model B is shown with a Dain push-rake. *Deere Archives*; The Model 830 was available only as a standard tread diesel tractor. *Deere Archives*.

Printed and bound in the United States of America

Contents

Acknowledgments

Special thanks to the following John Deere tractor owners: John Albrecht, Raymond Armistead, Dick Brockwoldt, Larry Goodwin, Bob Jensen, Don Klein, and Neil West, whose tractors were photographed at the Grand Detour Two-Cylinder Days.

John and Jon Davis, Walter and Bruce Keller, Lyle Pals, Orv Rothgarn, and Don Wolf, collector-restorers visited by Andrew Morland and me on our 1993 and 1994 photographic junkets.

And to Dr. Leslie Stegh, Head of the Deere & Company Library and Records Retention Department, and his staff, for their help and patience in collecting and printing all the Deere-supplied photographs, and for checking the text for glaring errors. Deere & Company stands alone in its field in catering to people interested in the historical aspects of the company and its products.

Introduction

This is the story of the first one hundred-fifty years of a great American institution: Deere & Company. The story is mostly told in pictures; pictures provided by the Deere & Company archives and Dr. Leslie Stegh, Head of the Deere Library and Record Retention Department. These pictures span the time from the earliest days of photography to the present day. Also included are contemporary photos of expertly restored John Deere tractors, some taken by renowned English automotive photographer Andrew Morland.

Over the last century and a half, the words "John Deere" have come to be almost interchangeable with the word "tractor." Like the words "Kleenex," or "Frigidaire," the name has achieved instant recognition over the world, and not only in rural regions. But the truth is that the name "John Deere" has graced the finest of a large variety of other agricultural and industrial implements, as well. Photographs of many of these are also included to show how development occurred over the years.

It's important to realize that this book covers a large segment of Americana. When John Deere began his business, the buffalo still roamed over the western plains. Women wore high-laced boots and Sunday evening band concerts were held in the more civilized towns. What is more important, however, is that the people and machines pictured here helped to give America the look and sound it has today.

Robert N. Pripps

Next page
The Furrow is one of the official publications of Deere and Company. It is published in eleven languages around the world, and in 1995 will celebrate the centenary of its publication.

YEAR 1922 · THIRD NO. · VOL. XXVII

The FURROW

Chapter 1

Tilling the Prairies:
1837-1862

"The determination of the proprietors to improve rather than deteriorate
on their already acknowledged superiority of manufacturing will be
sufficient guarantee to all that every exertion will be made to furnish
promptly a superior article at a low figure."
John Deere

Attacking the Gumbo

Prairie is the term for a vast expanse of flat land covered with coarse grass. It comes from the French word meaning "extensive meadow." On the typical prairie the overall flatness is somewhat relieved by low hills and shallow river valleys, and groves of trees dot the landscape. Illinois, Wisconsin, Minnesota, and Iowa comprise most of the prairie in the United States, while Alberta, Manitoba, and Saskatchewan are the Canadian prairie provinces.

The prairie probably developed as the result of severe fires and drought, followed by a period of heavy rains. The coarse grass grew at such a rate that tree seedlings were overshadowed and choked out. Eventually, the matting of the grasses of previous seasons and the heavy root structure prevented anything else from getting a start.

Herbert Dicksee's painting "The Last Furrow," graphically shows the arduous nature of horse plowing.

The prairies were an awesome sight to travelers in the late eighteenth century. Humorist Garrison Keillor suggests that the early Norwegian immigrants, searching for the Great Lakes, settled in Minnesota because they mistook the endless billows of waving grass for Lake Michigan. This assumption may not be so far fetched. Harriet Martineau, the eighteenth century English writer, likened going out on the prairie to going out on Lake Michigan in a canoe. Others of the time wrote that the uncongenial climate, the vastness, the flatness, and the isolation spoiled the beauty.

Northern Illinois was also a land of immense prairies. While southern Illinois was well populated by the 1700s, the North was ignored despite the open lands. James Monroe, the architect of the Louisiana Purchase, wrote about the area that is now Illinois in a letter to President Thomas Jefferson. He said, "A great part of the territory is miserably poor, especially that between Lake Michigan and the Mississippi River. It consists of extensive plains, which have not had, and will not have a single bush on them, for ages."

Sticky gumbo soil was spawned by the thick bed of grass and roots as year after year of decay turned it into a bed of humus. It was black and rock-free and extended as far down as seven feet.

By the late 1830s, the benefits of prairie soil were being recognized. For the task of tilling this soil, the term "prairie-breaking" was coined. Many methods were tried, from starting prairie fires to plowing under the sod with huge breaker plows pulled by as many as eight yoke of oxen. After the thatch was finally overcome, periodic re-plowing was required to break up the clods of sod and to keep the prairie grass from starting again.

Crude iron plows had appeared in the Near East about 1000 B.C., but it wasn't until about 1700 A.D. that the cast-iron plow was known in

An Indian family watches a pioneer farmer plow the prairie with a team of eight oxen and a crude wooden plow.

the western world. Cast-iron is by nature rough and full of surface imperfections known as blowholes. It does not take a polish and is prone to rusting, which further pits the surface. Cast-iron plow makers added a leather pouch to their plows as standard equipment. Inside this leather pouch was a wooden paddle, not unlike a modern-day windshield ice scraper. In many cases, the plowman could only travel a few yards in gumbo before it was necessary to roll the plow on its side and scrape the "mud" from the moldboard.

Bessemer steel was first made commercially in the United States in 1864. Before that, steel cost about twenty-five cents per pound which was more than twice that of iron. Thus, while it was available throughout the nineteenth century, it was only used where its superior strength, or other properties, were essential.

John Deere's Family Tree

John Deere was eight years old when his father was lost in an unfortunate maritime accident. He had been a tailor, and his widow, Sarah Deere continued his business to support the family, but young John was soon earning money himself. His mother insisted that he attend Middlebury College when he became a young man, which he did for a time. John was bent toward the practical, however, rather than the theoretical, so he apprenticed himself to a blacksmith. The apprenticeship was completed in 1825. Afterward, Deere was employed as a blacksmith, either for others, or in shops of his own.

The early prairie farmer had to stop to scrape the moldboard of his cast-iron plow, sometimes every ten feet.

The porous surface of cast-iron caused the sticky gumbo soil to adhere to the plow surface.

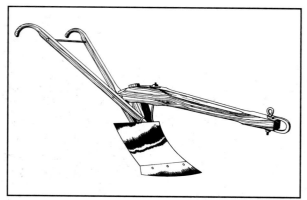

An artist's conception of John Deere's first plow based on how historians believe it was constructed. Deere fashioned the plow from a piece of polished steel from a broken saw blade. The smooth surface prevented the sticky gumbo soil from adhering, allowing the plow to scour. Although this picture shows a dividing line between the share (bottom) and the moldboard, some believe Deere's first several plows were one-piece, at least until the saw blade was used up.

In his own shops, in Leicester Four Corners and in Hancock, Vermont, John Deere began specializing in tool manufacture. His shovels, hoes, and pitchforks were known for their quality. Deere not only made tools to order, but made them to stock for later sale, thus gaining insight into the factory business.

In 1827, John Deere married Demarius Lamb from Granville, Vermont. By 1836, when John left for Illinois because of hard times in the East, they had four children and a fifth on the way. John followed a friend and business associate, Leonard Andrus, to the Illinois prairie town of Grand Detour, where the Rock River makes a sweeping horseshoe bend.

When John Deere arrived in Grand Detour, he was thirty-two years old. He had brought with him the necessary tools of his trade. These were soon put to use repairing a pitman arm on

John Deere's home in Grand Detour, Illinois, has been restored. It is on the grounds of the blacksmith shop. After John Deere got the shop running in 1837, he built the house and then sent for his family to come from Ver-

mont. When they arrived in 1838, John's wife was carrying their son, Charles, who was born after John left for Illinois. Charles was to play a big part in the future of John Deere's business. *Deere Archives*

John Deere's original blacksmith shop has been replicated by Deere & Company. The Grand Detour, Illinois, property is now a registered National Historical Landmark.

This is the interior of the reconstructed blacksmith shop of John Deere, as it would have been in the 1840s. John Deere's shop and home are a registered National Historic Landmark. The site and buildings were restored by Deere & Company. *Deere Archives*

Andrus' saw mill. It was in this mill that Deere spied a broken saw blade, and with a characteristic genius for responding to the needs of customers, his plow business was born.

Company History

Deere then did less and less of ordinary blacksmithing and more of the steel plows. These, at first, were the small plows the farmers used every spring and fall on land that had already been broken. As time went on, Deere developed new plow shapes and used combinations of cast iron, wrought iron, and steel in his plows.

Although the market for plows was good, cash money was scarce on the frontier. Banks were unreliable and cash flow problems began to plague John Deere. To ease this developing situation, Deere took on Leonard Andrus as a partner. Together, they built a new factory on the Rock River, leaving the blacksmith shop behind.

The firm was officially called Grand Detour Plow Company, however John Deere's name was on each plow. About ten people were employed, including Deere's nephew Samuel Charter Peek.

This W.H. Hinton painting shows the young John Deere shaping the piece of broken saw blade into the famous steel plow.

Another Hinton painting shows John Deere off to test his steel plow. Deere carved the wooden parts, as well as shaping the steel.

According to legend, farmers gathered to witness the first test of John Deere's first steel plow. This painting shows their elation when the plow proved it would scour.

The Peek name would play a part in the forthcoming events.

Again, financial problems required another partner and Horace Paine was taken in. The firm was now called L. Andrus & Company, reflecting Andrus' growing share. About two years later Paine was out and O.C. Lathrop was in. The company name was now Andrus, Deere and Lathrop and it was ten years after John Deere had arrived in Grand Detour. At this time, Francis Albert Deere, John's eighteen year old son, was taken into the business as a bookkeeper. Unfortunately, young Albert, as he was called, died before the year was out. It was not long before Lathrop was out of the firm, now again called Andrus & Deere. This arrangement, too was short lived, and Andrus and Deere split.

Obtaining materials at a reasonable cost had become a problem. Production was up to 1000 plows for the year. Although situated on the Rock River, Grand Detour was not afforded steamboat service except in periods of very high water. Thus, coal for the forges had to be brought in by wagon from LaSalle, some forty miles away. Steel and other metals came up the Mississippi from St. Louis, but had to be hauled overland to Grand Detour. Later that year, Deere announced his intentions to move the business to Moline, Illinois, on the Mississippi River.

In 1848, Deere moved his plow business to Moline, where he could get steel directly from St. Louis. Here again, different partnership arrangements were undertaken, with various degrees of success.

A variety of witnesses to the first test of John Deere's famous steel plow are shown in this painting by W.H. Hinton.

In 1853, John Deere's oldest surviving son, Charles (then sixteen) joined the firm, to remain with it for fifty-four years, until his death in 1907. Charles, who later followed his father as chief executive officer, had an inestimable influence on the success of the firm.

By 1853, the firm then known as "John Deere," annually produced about 4,000 plows plus various other implements. In just three more years, plow production jumped to almost 15,000, and the firm employed about seventy workers.

Financial difficulty again stalked John Deere in the "Panic of 1857." To stave off bankruptcy, for both the company and John Deere personally, reorganization was undertaken. New partners with cash were taken in. John Deere's assets were separated. Ownership of the company was now in the hands of four partners, of which twenty-one-year-old Charles Deere was principal. The Com-

John Deere brings out new plows for the traveler to load on his wagon in this early drawing of the Grand Detour operation.

John Deere moved his plow-making operation from Grand Detour to Moline in 1848. Moline was conveniently located on the Mississippi River; supplies such as steel and coal could be brought in by barge. Shown here is his first Moline factory building, the back of which was right on the river. Various versions of this picture show different dates on the front. In this case, 1837 is meant to indicate the beginning of the plow business.

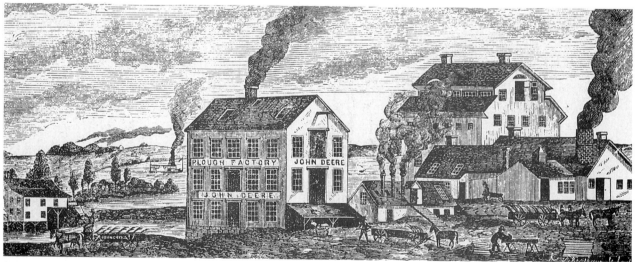

Another view of John Deere's Moline plow factory of 1847. In this illustration, the traveler's wagons, loaded with plows, heading off toward the east and west. Note the English spelling of "plough" on the side of the building.

pany was renamed "John Deere & Company."

The Civil War

As the war between the states began in America, Europe was hit by a year of crop failure. Weather in the prairie states and provinces was good, so the export market, plus food production to support the Yankee troops, made for good times for the prairie farmers. It was also a good time for implement makers, like Deere.

Only one member of the Deere family actually served in the war: James Chapman, husband of Jeannette Deere, one of John's daughters. Another of John's daughters, Emma, married Stephen Velie at this time. The Velie name would be a major part of the unfolding events.

By 1856, the company was producing more than just plows—agricultural implements were now included. The factory was still right on the river, and Rock Island was included in the location.

The reconstructed blacksmith shop in Grand Detour, Illinois, is now a registered National Historical Landmark. The shop has been restored to the way it was in the heyday of John Deere's blacksmith activities. The town, Grand Detour, was named for a sweeping bend in the Rock River, which flows by the town on its way to the Mississippi. *Deere Archives*

John Deere's celebrated plow factory, circa 1859. Construction of this factory, Deere's second in Moline, was begun in 1856. By 1859, production was up to approximately 15,000 plows per year.

An artist's conception of life in the plow shop of John
Deere, circa 1840.

This painting by W.H. Hinton, pictures John Deere holding his famous steel plow. In the background, 100 years
of progress are depicted, from opening the prairies in
1837 to tractor plowing with a rubber-tired John Deere
General Purpose Model A in 1937. *Deere Archives*

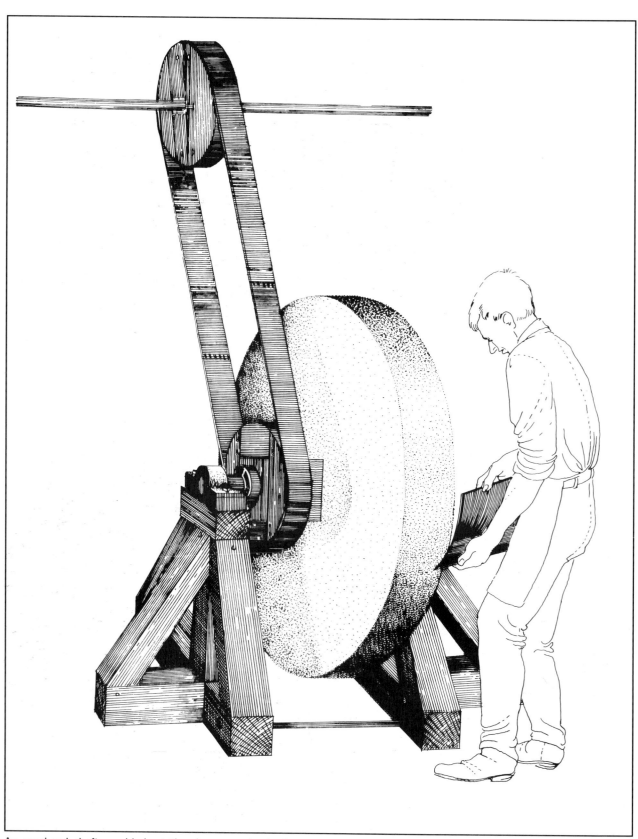

An overhead shaft provided rotational power prior to the
advent of electric motors. In John Deere's original plow
shop, the shaft was powered by a horse treadmill affair.

Charles Deere in about 1900. Charles was born in 1837 in Vermont shortly after his father had left for Illinois. He was a year old before he and his mother joined his father in Grand Detour. Charles started with the firm at age sixteen and took over day-to-day management at age twenty-one. His management style fostered independent branch houses that wielded much influence on the company and its products. He had been with the company for fifty-four years when he died at age seventy. After he died, his fellow board of director members made a formal resolution testifying "to his simple, strong, and manly character, and to his sterling worth."

Chapter 2

A Time for Expansion:
1863-1887

*"I will never, from this seventh day of February, Eighteen Hundred
and Sixty A.D., put my name to a paper that I do not expect to pay—
so help me God."*
Charles Deere

Charles Deere Takes Over

Charles Deere had taken over as chief executive of the company when he was just twenty-one years old. He was brought into the partnership in 1858 in a legal gambit to protect John Deere's personal assets from being attached by

Deere's first riding implement was the Hawkeye sulky corn cultivator introduced in 1863. It was also Deere's first departure from the plow business. Shown here is advertising copy for the Hawkeye.

New Deal Gang with Traction Engine.

Thus far no other manufacturer has produced a make-shift even for steam plowing which is capable of general or extended introduction. We were the first to construct a large gang of plows, and have to-day in the New Deal four, five and six-furrow gangs, the only plows of the kind that can successfully be used with an engine as motive power. By this addition to a steam equipment the latter can be employed in plowing two seasons, and yield with much larger profits and far less work for the operators than during the threshing season.

The necessary conditions are that the ground must be firm enough to stand the weight of the engine and fairly level so that steam may be safely kept in the boiler. The better the shape the ground is in for plowing the more satisfactory of course will be the results.

In operating, two men are necessary—one to run the engine and guide it so as to keep an even width of furrow, and one to manage the plow gang. No outfit of this kind is handy to handle at the ends of rows, or in turning corners, so that long furrows and large fields are desirable.

In hitching to an engine several links of heavy chain are necessary between the engine and the gang, so as to give slack enough to lift the plows out of the ground. An ordinary traction engine, either eight or ten horse, such as is to be found in every farming locality, will run a four, five or six-furrow New Deal Gang Plow with ease.

We guarantee the New Deals to do good work, but will of course give no warranty on the engine or power.

Send for special circular.

ORDER EXTRA SHARES BY NUMBER STAMPED ON BOTTOM OF EACH.

An advertisement for the Deere New Deal gang plow from the 1859 era. Note the caveats regarding the use of steam.

creditors. Once this maneuvering had accomplished its purposes, the partnership was dissolved. By the end of 1858, the business was solely in the hands of Charles Deere, although his father was never far from the action. Also before the end of 1858, Charles had invited his brother-in-law, Christopher Columbus Webber, to join the firm as a partner. Webber was married to Charles' older sister, Ellen. This arrangement, however, was short lived, as Webber had financial difficulties of his own and had to liquidate his share. For a time, the company used the official name Moline Plow Company. Unofficially, it was referred to as Deere & Company.

By the time the Civil War was over, Charles Deere had maneuvered the company through the troubled financial waters and was sailing smoothly. The name was officially changed to Deere & Company in 1864, and John was again listed as half owner. In actual fact, Charles ran the company and John tinkered in the shop. John Deere obtained some valuable patents for the company in those years.

Great advances in the 1860s in materials, especially steel, and in reduced material costs led the company to expand the product line. Patent rights for the Hawkeye sulky cultivator were obtained from its inventor, a Mr. W. Furnas. Ap-

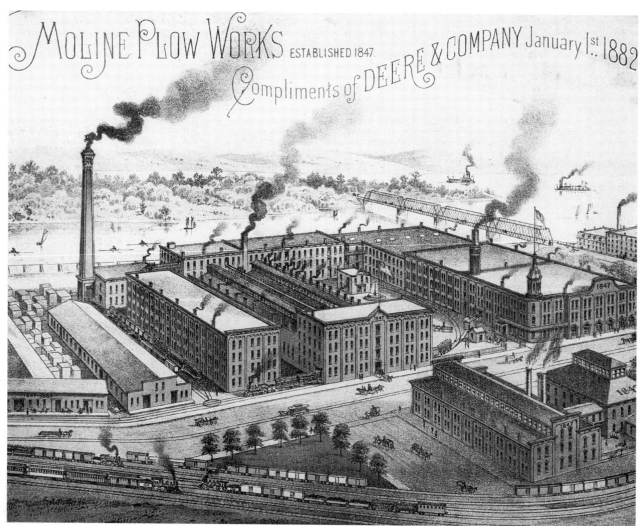

This calendar art from 1882 shows how the Deere Plow Works had grown. There are several interesting features in the picture: the horse-drawn trolley car (center), the train passing through the central building, the railroad turntable to divert cars between the buildings, and the diverse river traffic.

The Plow Works, as it appeared in 1867. Note the wagon-
load of plows.

The Plow Works in Moline, as it appeared just before the
turn of the century. The number of buildings has increased dramatically since the 1867 picture.

Charles Deere, at about age sixty, plows with a steel beam walking plow. Charles joined the company at age sixteen, and ran it from the age of twenty-one until he died at age seventy. Charles Deere's character marked Deere & Company perhaps to a greater extent than that of his father.

proximately 500 of these were sold in 1864, the first year they were in the catalog. Shop superintendent Gilpin Moore obtained a patent for a

How it used to be done. This old-time photo shows harvesting without even the use of the cradle scythe. This picture was used in Deere's magazine, *The Furrow*, to show the labor intensity of farming prior to the advent of machines.

similar sulky plow in 1870. The "Gilpin" sulky plow would prove to be very successful.

Incorporation

The company was apparently prospering in the 1860s, so what prompted the move from a partnership to a corporation is not known. On August 15, 1868, the firm became an Illinois corporation under the name of Deere & Company. Shareholders were John Deere, President; Charles Deere, Vice President; Stephen Velie; and George Vinton (related to John's wife). Within the year, Gilpin Moore and C.V. Nason (related to John's wife) were included with small shares. Charles Deere held 40 percent of the stock, and although he was listed as vice president, it was really his company. In 1869, Deere & Company delivered over 41,000 plows, harrows and cultivators.

Branch Houses

One of the outcomes of the Civil War was the expansion of the railroad transportation system. By the late 1860s, train transportation was becoming routine and reliable. Marketing now became regional, or even national, rather than local as it had been. Wholesalers, or "jobbers" sprang up in centers like Chicago, St. Louis and Dallas. Such outfits bought goods from the manufacturers at volume prices, and then either sold them themselves, or sold them to retailers at a mark-up. In either case, the jobber was required to cover the cost of transportation and storage of the goods until they were sold. Most jobbers handled several related lines, such as fruits and vegetables, or several brands of home furnishings.

The expanding farm implement companies tried distribution of their wares through jobbers, but the desired results were not being obtained. Much of this equipment required demonstration. Further, if loyalty to a particular brand was to translate into sales of more products to the same farmer, the jobber was not the one to do the selling. It mattered little to him which brand of harrow or plow was purchased by a farmer.

To obtain distribution and retain customer loyalty that had been built up by traveling salesmen, Charles Deere instituted a system of semi-company owned branch houses. The first was in Kansas City. It was jointly owned by the directors of Deere & Company and Alvah Mansur, a St. Louis businessman. Other houses were instituted with similar financial arrangements in St. Louis, Minneapolis, Omaha, and San Francisco.

The branch houses were semi-autonomous. They could handle equipment manufactured by others (even competitive items), and themselves engage in manufacturing proprietary items of farm equipment. The Deere & Mansur branch developed their own line of planters. Sales territories were never very well defined, and some conflicts between the branch houses arose. Travelers (traveling salesmen) from the home office in Moline, also occasionally infringed on branch house sales, but generally, the system worked well and the company prospered.

The Deere & Company product catalog of 1880 listed plows, cultivators, planters, harrows,

During the Civil War, the Plow City Rifle Company was made up of men from Moline, many of whom had worked at Deere & Company. Note the Deere riding plow in this photo, taken in 1865.

and wagons and buggies. There were several varieties of each; for example, the plow line included walking and riding plows, and single and gang plows.

John Deere Dies

After incorporation of the company, John Deere's role was minimal. Nevertheless, John Deere remained active. He was on the board of one of Moline's banks, and served a term as mayor of Moline. He also had some farm land that he tended himself.

In 1866, Demarius Lamb Deere, John Deere's wife and the mother of his nine children, died at age sixty. Later that year, John returned to the Lamb homestead in Vermont to commiserate with the family. While there, he became reacquainted with Demarius' maiden sister, Lucenia. When John Deere returned to Moline, he brought Lucenia with him as his new wife.

John Deere was one of a number of remarkable entrepreneurs who revolutionized agriculture in the nineteenth and twentieth centuries. In addition to Deere, Daniel Massey, C.H. McCormick, J.I. Case, James Oliver, Henry Ford, and Harry Ferguson were giants among the big industrialists of their times. All were self-educated and each started his own company and enlisted the support he needed to succeed.

On May 17, 1886, John Deere died at the age of eighty-two. His funeral in Moline was attended by 3,000 people. A floral plow graced the coffin with "John Deere" on the beam. Although he held some important patents, John Deere was not noted as an inventor, he was certainly not a financial genius, nor was he an exceptionally diplomatic leader. He did have, however, the charismatic characteristics known to many self-made people. He was a man of great personal bearing and dignity. He personified the company's integrity and dedication to quality. His name still graces the finest farm and industrial equipment.

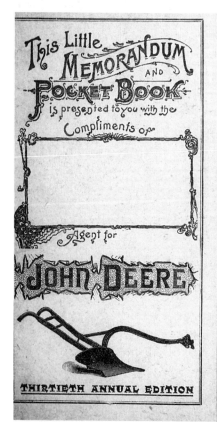

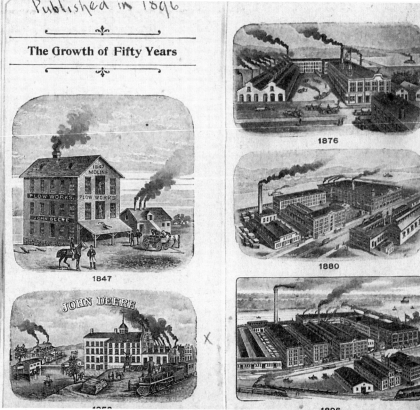

A complimentary memo book, published by Deere in 1896 for presentation by agents to customers, shows in five views, how the company had grown in fifty years.

Alvah Mansur, who formed Deere, Mansur & Company, with Charles Deere. Located in Kansas City, it was the first independent branch house for marketing Deere products.

Stephen Velie

Next page
The John Deere Secretary Disk Plow of 1890. It was so
named for the Secretary of Agriculture, who had asked for
a plow that would not pack the soil.

SECRETARY — SINGLE — REAR VIEW

For a quarter of a century the revolving disk has been known as the best means of cutting and turning the soil. but the difficulty of keeping it at a uniform depth in the ground and in a straight line of progression. setting as it does at an angle to the furrow, has prevented any general success of it as a plow for opening up and turning the furrow.

We have been experimenting in this line some years, and have at last hit upon a hook-shaped tine which penetrates the soil, pulling the disk any desired depth and holding it to a straight furrow line.

In this we claim an invention of rare merit, and its operation has only to be seen to commend it.

This new implement. which we now place on the market, is the outcome of a demand emphasized by the Secretary of Agriculture, who asks that a plow shall be invented that shall not leave the earth over which it passes so impacted by pressure as do the plows now in use.

In shallow tillage, with a cut say four inches in depth, the leverage of the plow point against the earth, the whole weight or power of the team producing a downward pressure at the cutting edge of share. leaves the base of the furrow that is turned over smooth and hard. In fact, it renders it almost impervious to water. Therefore, when a torrential rainfall comes upon land thus plowed and lying upon a land slope, the wash is enormous, and all the good surface earth is carried away. Furthermore, the water being unable to percolate through the subsoil, drains off and leaves the subsoil dry and hard.

By the use of the "Secretary" the ground is left in an entirely different condition. The disk scoops out the furrow, and in throwing it over thoroughly pulverizes it. The bottom of the furrow is left by the disk in its thoroughly natural condition ; that is, there has been no downward pressure on or sliding over of the surface to make it hard and smooth. The penetrating point, which runs under the disk, thoroughly breaks and stirs up the subsoil, and leaves it in the best possible condition to receive and retain moisture. The result is that in very heavy rains, the water, instead of running off, will sink down into the subsoil, and when the dry weather comes on will be drawn up to supply moisture to the plants.

This giant railroad plow was used for ditching along the tracks. Also displayed is a standard wood-beam walking plow and several model plows. Note the strange "deer" emblem under the man's elbow.

A car load of wood-beamed walking plows, circa 1882, is ready to roll. The sign says to return the car and rig to Deere And Co., Moline, Ill.

Chapter 3

The Modern Company:
1888-1912

"There is one thing you should not allow your travelers to forget . . .
their first duty is to get the plow trade."
C.C. Webber

Organization

Charles Deere had continued his decentralization via branch houses, but with centralized production and development. This was his consistent policy during the second half of the nineteenth century. He had surrounded himself with trusted compatriots who worked well with him. Stephen Velie Sr., the corporate secretary, handled financial matters and was the one who always counseled conservatism and caution. Gilpin Moore was his resident inventor and manufacturing man. Charles Nason ran the woodworking shop. George Vinton acted as general agent. Alvah Mansur and Lucius Wells were co-partners in the St. Louis and Omaha branch houses respectively. Charles C. Webber, the son of the late Christopher Webber, co-partnered the Minneapolis branch house. C.C. Webber, as he was called, had his ear to the ground as far as customers' needs went. He also had the ear of "Uncle Charles" Deere. Later in the century, when Stephen Velie Sr. died, Charles Deere brought up his son-in-law, William Butterworth, to be the corporate financial man.

The branch houses continued to press the home office to expand the product line, and this was done. The Gilpin sulky plow, however, continued to be a mainstay, remaining in the catalog until well after the First World War. Other types of walking and riding tillage equipment rounded out the line. It was in the last decade of the nineteenth century that tractor plows were added. Also added were plows designed especially for various areas of the country and a giant railroad plow to be used for ditching tracks.

In 1879, Charles Deere and Alvah Mansur formed a separate Moline company to manufacture corn planters. Later, other types of planters were added. Deere & Mansur Company also brought out stalk-cutters and hay rakes. Most of this equipment was labeled "Deere" and sold through the branch houses: a rather strange, but apparently workable arrangement. This manufacturing arrangement was used in subsequent situations, as well. The probable reason for it was not to dilute Deere ownership of John Deere's company. By making Deere & Mansur separate, Mansur's capital was used, but not mixed in with the family holdings. In financial dealings after the death of John Deere, those responsible for the company exhibited great concern for John Deere's reputation and fortune.

Wagons and Buggies

The Deere & Company catalog for 1880 included both wagons and buggies, but the full impact of that trade was not realized for another decade. In 1881, Mr. Morris Rosenberg, presi-

An 1897 Deere & Company advertisement touts the John Deere line of "plow goods." The line, at this time, included plows, harrows, listers, and cultivators.

Holt was a pioneer in the combine field, having sold their first unit in 1886. After Holt and Best merged to form Caterpillar in 1929, combines were made by their Western Harvester Division in Stockton, California. Western's line was made available to Deere in 1935 as part of a reciprocal arrangement in which Deere dealers would offer Caterpillar crawlers and Caterpillar dealers would offer Deere wheel tractors.

dent of the Moline Wagon Company, bought an interest in the Omaha/Council Bluffs branch operation and began selling wagons through that dealership. This led to links to the other branch houses, and soon trade was so profitable that Moline Wagon was acquired by Deere & Company.

The St. Louis branch, under Mansur, carried a full line of buggies. In 1889, Mansur, and his branch manager, George Tebbetts, formed a company to manufacture buggies of their own.

These too, were distributed by the other branch houses.

Bicycles

The "Safety Bicycle" was invented in about 1880. This was a cycle with both wheels the same size, propelled by pedals, sprockets, and chains. During the next decade the design matured, with ball bearings, coaster brakes, and pneumatic tires. The bicycle's popularity in the U.S. peaked in the last ten years of the century.

The John Deere bicycle of 1890. In the last decade of the nineteenth century, a bicycle craze swept the country. Board members C.C. Webber and Charles Deere Velie were instrumental in getting Deere involved. Velie organized the "Deere Road Race," a twenty mile competition.

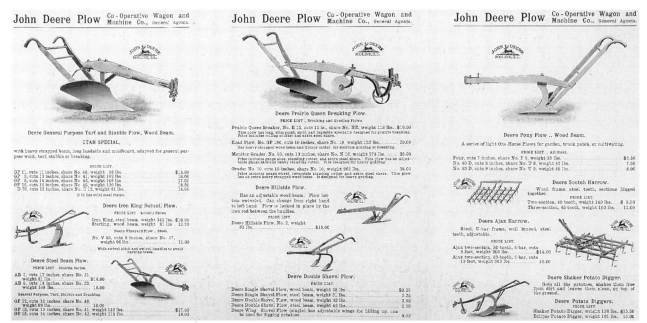

These pages from a 1901 brochure include a variety of "plow goods" with prices. Deere plows were never the low-price line, but sales were made on high quality and extra material strength.

This rare photograph from 1892 shows the tractor devised by John Froelich, from Froelich, Iowa. Froelich's tractor was the first to propel itself both backwards and forwards, and to both pull an implement and power it with a flat belt. The implement was the big Case thresher shown in the background. Froelich pulled the thresher from farm to farm in the Langford, South Dakota, area.

He thus completed a fifty-day threshing run and threshed some 72,000 bushels of grain. Investors from Waterloo were impressed enough to put up the finances and join with Froelich to form the Waterloo Gasoline Traction Engine Company, which built the famous Waterloo Boy tractor. The Waterloo Boy was acquired by Deere & Company in 1918.

Over four million people rode bicycles regularly. In this time before the automobile, people got their first taste of wheeled mobility.

Surprisingly, C.C. Webber was the main catalyst to get Deere involved in the "great bicycle craze." Webber, who cautioned that the plow business was the main business, and that the shoemaker should stick to his last, was the first to introduce bikes at the Minneapolis branch.

Charles Deere Velie, was also an enthusiast, organizing "The Deere Road Race" over a twenty mile course near Minneapolis.

At first, several brands of bicycles were handled by the branch, but in 1895 it had manufactured under the Deere company name three of its own bicycles. The three were the "Leader," the "Roadster," and the "Moline Special." By then, the other branch houses were also taking

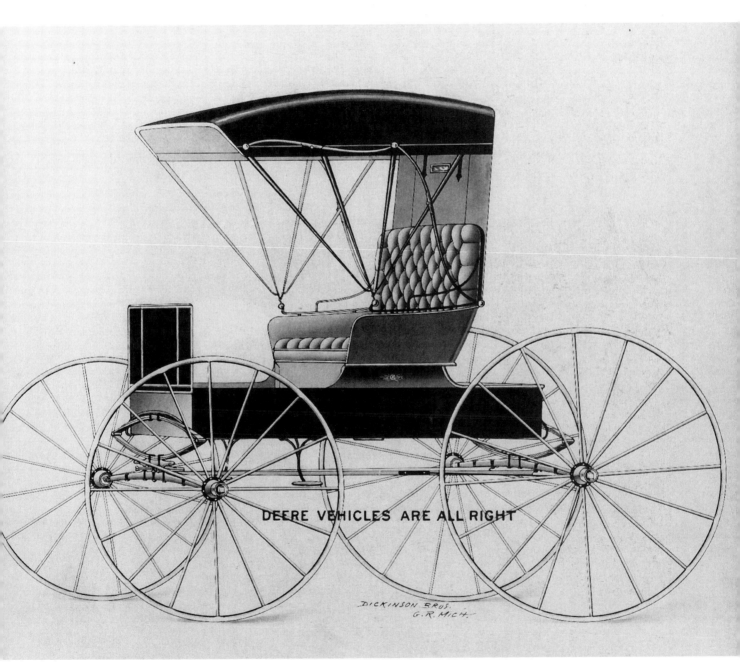

DEERE VEHICLES ARE ALL RIGHT

DICKINSON BROS.
G.R. MICH.

Deere & Company got into the buggy business in 1891 when it acquired Mansur and Tebbitts, of St. Louis, Missouri. Shown here is a two-seater with double transverse leaf springs. Note the slogan: "Deere Vehicles Are All Right."

up the trade. Charles Velie went so far as to develop a bicycle trademark, showing a deer riding a bicycle, the implication being that even the deer would be left behind without the bike.

The bicycle craze was over as rapidly as it had started. By 1900, Deere was no longer carrying bicycles in their catalogs and had ceased production.

Harvesters

The years 1896 and 1897 saw a severe recession in America, especially in the agriculture equipment business. The latter was due in large extent to over production, drastic competition, and devastating price wars. Companies reacted by merging to eliminate competition as the economy recovered from the recession. Between 1898 and 1902, 212 consolidations occurred, almost twice the number occurring in the preceding nine years.

Two harvesting dynasties, McCormick and Deering, now became serious about merging

their two companies. Deering proposed a two-step merger. Each family should buy minority interest in the other firm. Then, together, they would acquire three other competitors: Plano Manufacturing of Chicago; Warder, Bushnell & Glessner of Springfield, Ohio; and Milwaukee Harvester Company of Milwaukee, Wisconsin.

The McCormicks, still the strongest, balked at any suggestion of loss of control. The merger efforts almost stalled until one George W. Perkins, a J. P. Morgan partner and adviser to the McCormicks, proposed a ten-year stock trust. The trust would hold all the stock of the new International Harvester Company, with Perkins, McCormick, and William Deering's son Charles serving as trustees.

Thus on July 28, 1902, International Harvester Company was born. The name, picked by George Perkins, was selected to reflect its global scope. Harvester, as it came to be called, controlled 85 percent of U.S. grain harvester production and boasted assets of 110 million dol-

Another Deere buggy with a deer in harness from 1899 art, probably for a calendar. The Deere factory in Moline is shown in the background, although Deere buggies were made in St. Louis.

1847.

1884.

1856.

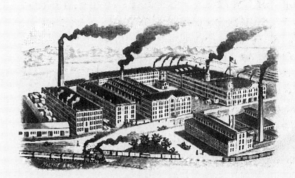

1888.

1876.

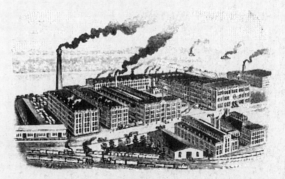

1894.

1880.

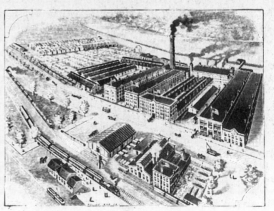

1897.

lars, a staggering amount in 1902. Included were malleable iron works, twine factories, timber lands and sawmills, hemp properties, coal and iron mines, the Illinois Northern Railway, plus the plants in Chicago, Milwaukee, and Springfield, Ohio.

Needless to say, the merger of these companies got the attention of the Deere board of directors. When the new International Harvester company began adding lines of tillage implements, wagons, spreaders, gasoline engines, and even tractors, the board became worried. With such a powerful full-line company vying for the hearts and minds of the independent dealer organizations, it was time to act. One of these dealers was Joseph Dain Manufacturing, which also made haying equipment for Deere branches. In

1904, Harvester launched itself into the hay equipment business and the fat was in the fire. A short time later, Deere hired away from International Harvester Mr. Harry Podlesak, a binder/harvester designer, and Mr. A.C. Funk, a manufacturing expert. A harvester plant was built in Moline. By 1911, Mr. Funk's health was failing, and Joseph Dain took over management of the plant. International Harvester had counterattacked by marketing a line of plows.

The Death of Charles Deere

On October 29, 1907, the seventy-year-old Charles Deere died after a lingering illness of about five years. He had been with the company for fifty-four years. A formal eulogy was appended to the board minutes conveying affection and admiration. It said, in part: "We who were his associates for many years thus record our regard and testify to his simple, strong and manly character, and to his sterling worth."

Charles Deere's son-in-law, William Butterworth, had been brought along by Charles as his

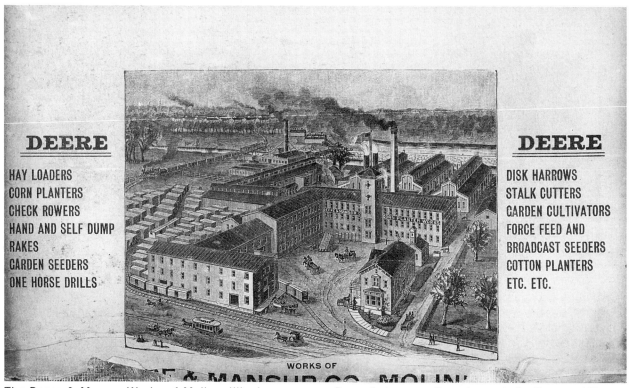

The Deere & Mansur Works of Moline, Illinois, was shown in the 1891-92 Rock Island–Moline City Directory. Although the Deere Plow Works and the Mansur Works were separate companies, they were closely related.

Deere dealers were the sole agents for Deere and Mansur planters. By the time of this directory, the product line had grown from just corn planters.

heir apparent. The board promptly elected him President.

The Modern Company

In January of 1910, the directors of Deere & Company made a resolution that all factories and distribution houses should be unified. This remarkable undertaking was mainly accomplished by the first half of 1911. All the branch houses, with their separate ownership, were brought into the fold. Dain Manufacturing and Deere & Mansur were purchased by Deere & Company. Other companies with related capabilities were also purchased, including an important one for the future: Van Brunt Manufacturing Company of Horicon, Wisconsin. The name Deere, or John Deere, was to be applied to all products of the reformulated company. In Deere internal circles, the company after 1911 was referred to as the "Modern Company."

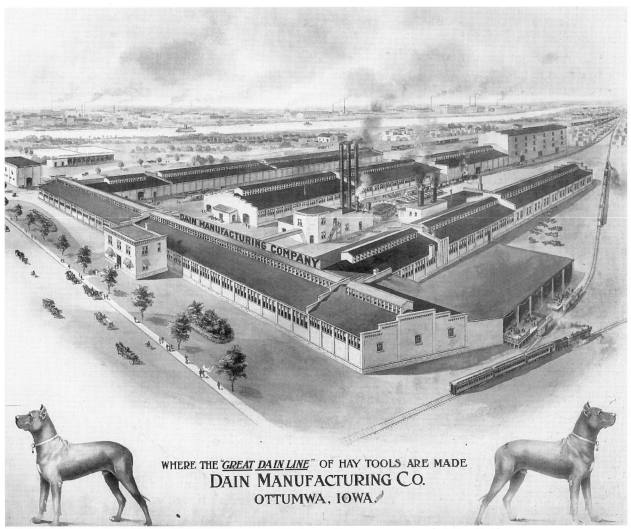

WHERE THE *GREAT DAIN LINE* OF HAY TOOLS ARE MADE
DAIN MANUFACTURING CO.
OTTUMWA, IOWA.

Joseph Dain sold his furniture business in 1882 to pursue his ideas for streamlining the process of hay making. The business was incorporated in 1890 with Dain as president and the factory located in Carrollton, Missouri. By 1895, an alliance was made with Deere & Company's Kansas City branch house for the sale of Dain's haying equipment. At the turn of the century, Dain had moved to Ottumwa, Iowa. A subsidiary, Dain Manufacturing Company, Limited, was located in Welland, Ontario, to serve the vast Canadian market. Joseph Dain became a vice president and board member of Deere & Company when his companies were taken over by Deere in the reorganization of 1910.

Joseph Dain, Sr., shown here in 1910 at the time of the sale of his companies to Deere. Dain had been a successful furniture man in Meadville, Missouri, but became interested in improving the process of hay making by the use of sweep rakes. His idea was to sweep up the hay right from the cut swath with a device that looked like a big slotted dust pan. The device could also be used for stacking the hay directly, for outdoor storage. After Dain became a member of the board of Deere & Company, he was given the assignment of developing Deere's first tractor. The result of his effort was known as the Dain all-wheel drive John Deere. Although fifty were sold to customers, the tractor's price was about double the planned $700. Two other factors in 1918 prevented the success of an otherwise very good machine: Dain died suddenly, and Deere & Company bought the Waterloo Boy tractor outfit.

Four men pose with a sulky plow they are assembling at the John Deere Moline Plow Works. The photo was taken in about 1900.

This is the factory scene at the turn of the century. Note the wood block floor, the overhead shafts and drive pulleys, and the hand carts for in-shop transportation. Also note the exposed electric wires in the upper right corner. This photo was taken in 1910 at the John Deere Harvester Works forge shop.

Hand plowing with a team was an arduous task even under the best of circumstances. This 1908 photo shows good conditions of level, rock-free ground and turf that is thick, but not too deep. Trees on the horizon help the plowman keep the furrows straight; straight furrows are the mark of a good plowman. Henry Ford, the auto magnate, was quoted as saying, "I have walked many a weary mile behind a plow and I know the drudgery of it."

John Deere got into the wagon business through association of its independent branch houses with the Moline Wagon Company. When the company reorganized in 1910, Moline Wagon Company was merged. It was then known as the John Deere Wagon Works. Deere produced a variety of wagons and wagon gear up to modern times.

Van Brunt was an old-line seed drill company when it was acquired by Deere in 1912. The Van Brunt Manufacturing Company was founded in 1860 in Mayville, Wisconsin, but in 1861, it was moved to Horicon, Wisconsin; the present site of Deere's Commercial Products Division. This photo shows the Van Brunt plant in about 1910.

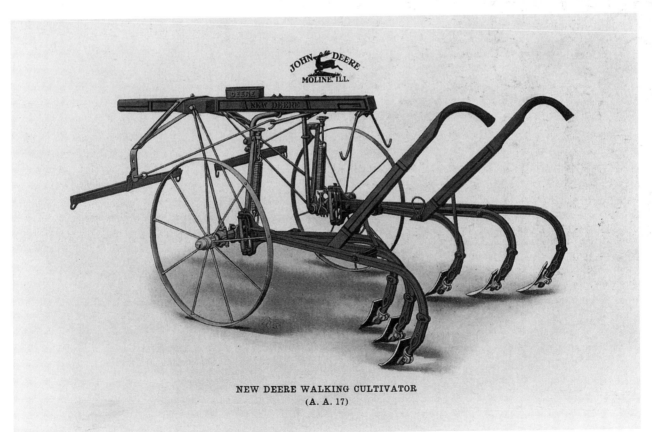

NEW DEERE WALKING CULTIVATOR
(A. A. 17)

A studio picture of the New Deere Walking Cultivator, taken for a 1910 advertisement. Deere's first venture into the manufacture of implements other than plows was in 1858 with this cultivator. By 1910, they America's largest producer of cultivators.

JOHN DEERE TWO-WAY SULKY PLOW

The John Deere Two-way Sulky Plow of 1910 is shown in this studio photo. Two-way plows were used so that all the sod rolls would be in the same direction, avoiding the "dead furrow" in the center of the field.

NEW DEERE LIGHT DRAFT SULKY

John Deere Sulky plows were all related to the Gilpin plow of the 1870s, invented by Deere board member and factory supervisor, Gilpin Moore. Not simple devices, sulky plows were drawn by the harness traces pulled at the lower clevis through an evener. The upper wooden beam that went between the horses served to steer the plow. In the case of the plow shown here, steering was through the tail wheel. In others, a front wheel did the steering. Springs were used to aid in lifting the plow and in adjusting the land wheel. Shown here is a 1910 New Deere Light Draft Sulky Plow.

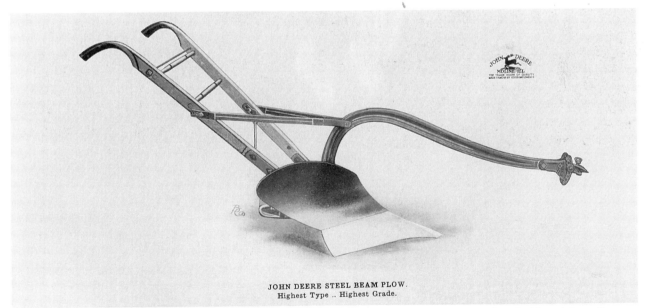

JOHN DEERE STEEL BEAM PLOW.
Highest Type .. Highest Grade.

As stated by Christopher Columbus Webber, Deere board member and branch house manager at the turn of the century, the first duty of the traveling salesmen was to get the plow trade. At least until the advent of the tractor, Deere & Company was known as a plow company. From the first crude John Deere plow fashioned from the saw blade, the walking plow progressed to the steel beam plow shown in this 1936 ad photo. This same plow was shown in catalogs as early as 1899.

Burton Peek.

Chapter 4

A Time for Tractors:
1913-1937

"I think it is safe to eliminate the horse, the mule, the bull
team, and the woman, so far as generally furnishing motive
power is concerned."
W.L. Velie, 1918

Big Four to Dain

Steam began providing farm power around the middle of the nineteenth century. In fact, John Deere provided a gang plow for a steamer made by J.W. Fawkes in 1858. It was one of the first successful mechanized plows in America. But in the 1890s, the remarkable gasoline engine was on the scene. It was quickly adapted to the

By 1913, large-acreage farmers were using steam tractors to good effect. Shown here is a John Deere twelve-bottom gang plow being pulled by a big steamer. The problem with the steam engines was obtaining fuel for them; naturally, a 50hp or 60hp engine took a substantial amount. The traction engine shown is apparently powered by coal. As can be seen from the photo, wood for fuel in this locale was out of the question. Straw was often used, but copious amounts were required. The difficulty in obtaining fuel was the impetus for gasoline-kerosene tractors.

many back breaking, monotonous jobs around the farm; jobs such as pumping water for animals, grinding feed, and shelling corn. It was not long before the ingenious farmer was substituting the gas engine for steam in jobs where steam had been king for fifty years.

The first gasoline traction engines, as they were then called, were little more than gas engines mounted on steam engine running gear. The first recorded production tractor was the 1889 Charter. Only six were built. The Charter was a 15hp gas engine mounted on a Rumely steam engine chassis.

In 1891, The William Deering Company mounted their two-cylinder 6hp engine on a New Ideal mower, making it self-propelled. For the next several years, Deering, who had not yet merged with McCormick to form International Harvester, made several other self-propelled farm machines, but not tractors per se.

In 1892, John Froelich of Froelich, Iowa, mounted a Van Duzen engine on a Robinson steam running gear. The machine had an operator's platform in front, a steering wheel, and could propel itself backward and forward. The 20hp engine operated on gasoline. Froelich, during the 1892 harvest season, employed the machine in a custom threshing operation lasting fifty days. He both pulled and powered a Case 40x58 thresher, threshing some 72,000 bushels of small grain. A year later, Froelich was instrumental in forming the Waterloo Gasoline Traction Engine Company, of Waterloo, Iowa.

The early efforts of the Waterloo Gasoline Traction Engine Company did not, however, pay off in the first commercially-viable internal com-

A Twin-City "40" plows with a John Deere gang plow in 1913. The Twin-City appeared in Deere export catalogs of about that time.

bustion (IC) tractor. That honor goes to two men named Charles, of Charles City, Iowa: Charles Hart and Charles Parr. The Hart-Parr company made their first tractor in 1902

After the formation of International Harvester in 1902, work on tractors accelerated. Harvester was among the first of the long-line implement companies to offer a tractor; their first being introduced in 1906. Their first unit typifies the problems of the time, as its single-cylinder engine was mounted on rollers so that it could be moved back and forth to engage a fric-

A Case 10-20 of 1913 pulls a three-bottom Deere plow at 2mph plowing speed. Note the tall air intake pipe; an effort to get clean air for the engine before the development of air cleaner filters.

Willard Velie, a Deere board member, introduced a resolution to the Deere board in 1912 to build a proprietary tractor. This was surprising, since Velie, himself, had a tractor company. This photo shows the Velie 12-24 handling a three-bottom John Deere plow.

The Big Four Gas Tractor, with a John Deere seven-bottom plow, won the 1910 Winnipeg Trials. Several years after, the Atlanta and St. Louis branches pictured the Big Four in their catalogs as a Deere product. Deere directors attempted to buy the Big Four outfit, but Big Four sold out to Emerson Brantingham instead.

tion drive. The engine had an open crankcase and employed spray-tank cooling. In 1908, the public got its first opportunity to compare various brands of steam and IC tractors in head to head competition. That year, and for several following, the Winnipeg Industrial Exposition featured tractor trials. Engineers and mechanics from the manufacturers made their machines perform for the worldwide press and for farm observers. The first year, all entrants used Canadian Cockshutt plows. In subsequent years, the tractor maker could choose his plow brand. All chose either Cockshutt or John Deere plows, except for Inter-national Harvester. They picked a Parlin & Orendorff. This fact did not escape Deere & Company management. Harvester had just embarked in the hay equipment business. Deere had taken on harvesters in retaliation. It was not long before Harvester bought the plow maker Parlin & Orendorff.

For the 1910 Winnipeg competition, the "over 30hp" class was won by the Gas Traction Company of Minnesota using a John Deere seven-bottom plow. Gas Traction made a unique tractor called the Big Four. Big it was, at 19,000lb, it had drive wheels eight feet tall. And

Deere & Company board member, C.H. Melvin, was commissioned by the board to develop a tractor in 1912. This 1914 photo shows the results of his efforts. It was a three-wheel machine with two seats, so that it could be operated in either direction. The drive wheels went first for plowing and tilling. The opposite direction was used for pulling wagons and trailed implements. Durability of the Melvin tractor was poor, so efforts were halted in 1914.

it had a four-cylinder, 30hp engine. The success in the competition prompted Deere's St. Louis and Atlanta branch houses to list the Big Four in their catalogs and to refer to it as "Our Big Four Tractor." The Big Four is therefore considered by some to be Deere's first tractor.

The Deere board of directors was so impressed with the success of the arrangement they made an offer to buy the Gas Traction outfit.

Much to their surprise, the offer was rebuffed, and Gas Traction then sold out to Emerson Brantingham, of Rockford, Illinois. Emerson Brantingham continued the Big Four with improvements. The Rockford firm was later taken over by Case.

Deere & Company did joint marketing with the maker of the Twin City tractor and with Hart-Parr. Some branches even carried the

A Russell Giant kerosene tractor demonstrates with a John Deere ten-bottom plow. The Russell produced 30hp at the drawbar and 60hp on the belt pulley. Because of the market for large tractors in Canada, Russells were in demand.

The three-wheel, single wheel drive Bull tractor was introduced in 1913. It quickly garnered first place in tractor production, partly because of its $400 price. Although the Bull tractor was short-lived, the company developed into Toro, the lawn and garden implement company of today. The John Deere gang is shown here evaluating the Bull with a Deere sulky plow.

In 1914, the success of the small Bull tractor led the Deere & Company board to again commission a board member, Joseph Dain, to build an experimental tractor. The target price was $700 and it was to be a three-plow machine. Dain came up with a three-wheel, all-wheel drive machine that was definitely ahead of its time. Unfortunately, the selling price was closer to $1,200 than $700. When the Waterloo Boy outfit became available, the Dain tractor was dropped. Shown here is an early experimental model.

Deering self-propelled mower, but such cooperation with International Harvester was discouraged by the board.

In 1912, Willard Velie, board member and grandson of John Deere, introduced a resolution to the board to produce a proprietary tractor. Despite reservations by the new president, William Butterworth, the resolution was passed unanimously. Mr. C.H. Melvin was given the job of designing and building a prototype.

Melvin came up with an interesting design using a four-cylinder engine of about 30hp. It was mounted directly over two large drive wheels. On the opposite end was a smaller, single wheel, which was steerable from a vertical steering post and wheel. Two operator seats were provided; one facing in each direction of travel on opposite sides of the steering post. For plowing, the engine end went first. For all other work, the small, or steering, wheel went first. The operator merely switched seats for each case. Three plows were mounted underneath. To raise them, a unique power lift was invented.

Butterworth's reluctance to commit large amounts of cash to tractor development were based both on Deere's philosophy of concentrating on the plow business and on what had happened to other tractor makers. Rumley, for example, had been left with mountains of uncollectable debt by crop failure in Canada. Nevertheless, Deere's decision whether to manufacture the Melvin tractor was made for them by the tractor itself. Its performance and durability were disappointing. Only one example was built, and by 1914, all work was stopped.

Next, board member Joseph Dain was asked to come up with a tractor. Fairly restrictive boundaries were placed on the project: the target

The Dain-John Deere in almost final form. The tractor performed well and had adequate power and traction. About fifty were actually sold to customers under the John Deere trademark, Which makes the Dain the first John Deere tractor. By 1917, Henry Ford had launched his Fordson; the Deere board was apprehensive of competitive forces that the auto magnate could bring to the market, and so elected to buy the Waterloo Boy tractor company, instead of developing the Dain machine.

selling price was $700 (the Big Four had sold for $3,000), and it was to be small. In 1913, an outfit called the Bull Tractor Company introduced a small 12hp, single wheel-drive tractor selling for around $400. This trim, agile little machine became first in sales (displacing International Harvester) by 1914. Although its popularity did not last long (the concept was not mechanically sound), it did spawn a subsidiary still around today: Toro, the lawn, garden, and golf course equipment maker.

The success of the little Bull tractor was what the Deere board had in mind. The thought of farmers owing on a tractor for three or four seasons did not seem reasonable to the board, either, as a bad crop year was a likelihood in that amount of time. Nevertheless, Dain thought he could meet the board's challenge.

Dain came up with a very interesting design. It was an all-wheel drive, three-wheeled machine, with two wheels in front and one in the rear. The front wheels were steering wheels, as well as drivers. It weighed only 4,600lb, but had a drawbar pull of over 3,000lb. It was capable of handling a three-bottom plow. Unfortunately, the costs indicated the price of the tractor would have to be in the order of $1,200, rather than $700. Most board members felt, however, that the tractor should sell at that price.

Various prototypes were built and tested in several areas of the country. Glowing reports came back indicating this was the most capable tractor on the market. Dain was detailed to work up a powered cultivator along the same lines as the tractor, to be called the "Tractivator." This, too was accomplished and proved successful in

Max Sklovsky was head of the Deere & Company design department and Chief Engineer. He is shown here on his three-wheel tractor which was developed at the same time as the Dain machine, and was similar to the Dain, but smaller. It could claim the first unitized frame design. It was steered by a swing-axle arrangement, obviating the need for individual wheel universal joints. This photo was taken in 1916.

operation. Still, the board withheld the go-ahead for volume production. William Butterworth was the main holdback.

Finally, a go-ahead was given to make and sell 100 production tractors, to be assembled by an outside firm. Two months later, Joseph Dain died of pneumonia following a trip to the testing field. With him died much of the push for the tractor project. Besides, it was now 1917 and World War I was taking more and more production capacity. Also Henry Ford, of automobile fame, had recently launched a 2,700lb tractor. The board was leery of the marketing forces that Ford could bring to bear (and rightly so, as it lat-

er turned out). Frank Silloway, who headed sales while George Peek was in Washington on his war job, had heard that the Waterloo Engine Company was for sale. They were the maker of the capable, $700, Waterloo Boy Tractor; the heir of the first successful tractor made by Froelich in 1892. The board immediately dispatched Silloway to Waterloo to check it out.

Froelich to Waterloo Boy

Late in 1892, Froelich joined with others to form the Waterloo Gasoline Traction Engine Company. Four tractors of the Froelich design were built. Two of these were sold to customers.

At about the same time as the Dain tractor experiments, some efforts were made by the Deere Experimental Department to come up with a motorized cultivator. One example is shown in this 1915 photo.

Neither satisfied their purchasers and both were returned. To generate cash flow, the company developed a line of stationary engines. In 1895, the company reorganized and dropped the word "Traction" from its name. With the name change, Mr. Froelich also left the company. By 1906, six engine models were in production, which carried the trade name "Waterloo Boy." Tractor experiments continued, however. In 1911, a Mr. A.B. Parkhurst, from Moline, joined

The Model B horse-drawn single action disk was in the catalog from the turn of the century into the 1940s. It was originally marketed by Deere and Mansur.

the Waterloo Gasoline Engine Company, bringing with him three tractors of his own design, with two-cylinder engines.

From 1911 to 1914, many variations on the theme were tried. In early 1914 the Waterloo Boy Model R tractor was offered for sale. It was a four-wheel rear wheel drive machine, with one forward speed and one reverse. The engine was a two-cylinder type with a displacement of 333ci. It produced 25hp at the belt (the drawbar rating was 12).

The Model R was sold in thirteen styles, A through M, until 1918, the year Deere & Company purchased the firm. Style N, which became the Model N, was introduced in 1917 and produced until 1924.

World War I

The Waterloo Boy was an immediate success, and Deere was able to ease the price up to over $1200 in short order. Business was good during the years of World War I. Over 4000 Waterloo Boys were exported to England to aid in overcoming food shortages. English tractors used the brand name "Overtime" rather than Waterloo Boy. Deere sold more than 5,000 Waterloo

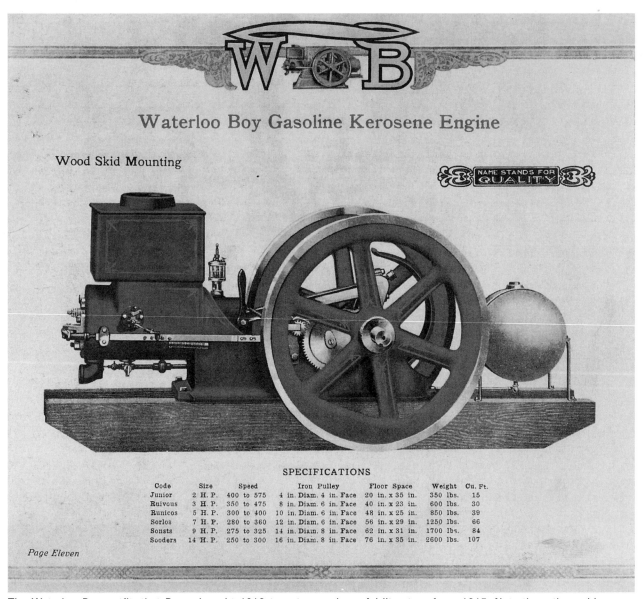

W⊙B

Waterloo Boy Gasoline Kerosene Engine

Wood Skid Mounting

NAME STANDS FOR QUALITY

SPECIFICATIONS

Code	Size	Speed	Iron Pulley	Floor Space	Weight	Cu. Ft.
Junior	2 H. P.	400 to 575	4 in. Diam. 4 in. Face	20 in. x 35 in.	350 lbs.	15
Ruivous	3 H. P.	350 to 475	8 in. Diam. 6 in. Face	40 in. x 23 in.	600 lbs.	30
Runicos	5 H. P.	300 to 400	10 in. Diam. 6 in. Face	48 in. x 25 in.	850 lbs.	39
Sorlos	7 H. P.	280 to 360	12 in. Diam. 6 in. Face	56 in. x 29 in.	1250 lbs.	66
Sonsts	9 H. P.	275 to 325	14 in. Diam. 8 in. Face	62 in. x 31 in.	1700 lbs.	84
Sooders	14 H. P.	250 to 300	16 in. Diam. 8 in. Face	76 in. x 35 in.	2600 lbs.	107

Page Eleven

The Waterloo Boy outfit, that Deere bought 1918 to get the Waterloo Boy tractor, also sold a variety of farm engines. Ad literature from 1915. Note the rather odd names under the heading "Code."

Boys in 1920, after the end of World War I. Henry Ford had begun producing his $750 Fordson tractor in earnest in 1918. By 1920, annual production was 67,000!

The Fordson was a 2,700lb tractor with 20 belt horsepower and 10 on the drawbar. It was in most respects a worthy tractor, especially for the price; about half that of the 25 belt/12 drawbar horsepower, 6,200lb Waterloo Boy.

A severe economic downturn surprised almost everyone in 1921. The agricultural industry was especially hard hit as over capacity due to the war caused equipment markets to become glutted. Deere had scheduled forty Waterloo Boys per day for the last half of 1921. In actual fact, they sold only seventy-nine tractors for the whole year! If this was a problem for Deere, Ford

had scheduled 300 Fordson tractors per day for 1921. Henry Ford knew what to do. He first cut the price to $620. Other tractor makers followed suit, including Deere. The Waterloo Boy price was cut to $890. So Ford further cut his price to $395; well below his cost. Ford managed to sell 35,000 Fordsons in 1921, and in 1922 sales were back to 67,000. And in 1923, over 100,000 were sold.

Only International Harvester had the strength to counter attack. As early as 1910, Harvester engineers had been interested in tractors that could do more than just pull trailed loads or drive loads with a flat belt. They had tested several variations of Motor-Cultivators. By 1919, the concept had become the general purpose "Farmall." In 1924, some 200 pre-produc-

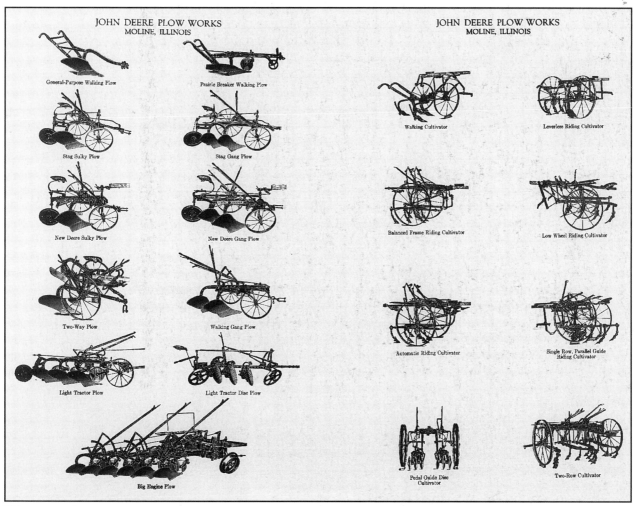

This page and next page
The 1918 Deere & Company product line as shown in the annual report for that year.

tion models were sold to customers. By 1926, the new Rock Island (Illinois) plant was in operation and Farmalls were rolling out the door.

Ford could see that the Fordson needed a complete redesign to be competitive with the Farmall and so transferred production to Ireland in 1927. International Harvester Company was clearly again at the top of the long-line farm implement industry. It enjoyed sales three times that of Deere & Company, its nearest competitor.

John Deere Tractors Model D and C

The Fordson challenge of 1921 caused the Deere Engineering department to look at the Waterloo Boy in comparison to other tractors. Before the Farmall, International Harvester had introduced a new 15-30 in 1921 and a 10-20 in 1922. Hart-Parr had come out with a new 12-25 and a 15-30 in 1918. All looked more like a Fordson than like a Waterloo Boy! They were smaller, and lighter, and they all had an engine hood like a car. Before Deere's acquisition, Waterloo Boy engineers had been working on a new tractor built after the fashion of the competition. Deere engineers quickly picked up on it and developed it.

Following the Waterloo Boy tradition of identifying variations with style letters, Deere built four test styles: A through D. When style D was selected for production, the label was changed to "Model D." It was introduced in 1923 and produced along with the Waterloo Boy. To say that the Model D was a success would be an understatement, as its production run of thirty years is the longest of any tractor model to date. It firmly established Deere as a maker of quality tractors.

Deere & Company knew they had to react to Harvester's dominance of the field of all-pur-

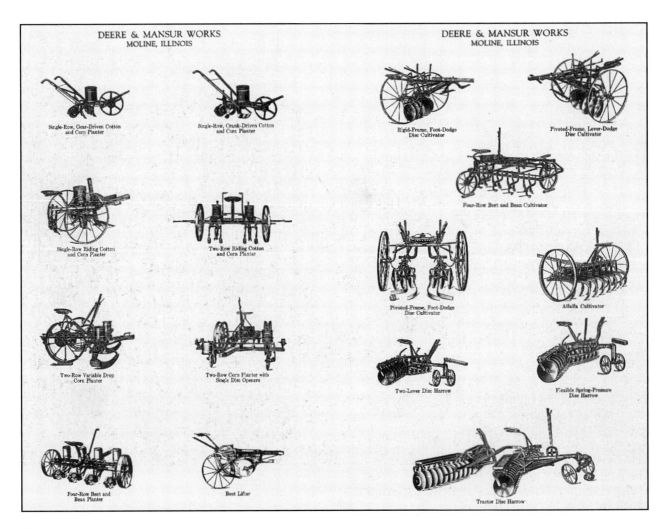

The Waterloo Boy Kerosene Tractor plant, in Waterloo,
Iowa, as it appeared at the time of the Deere & Company
purchase in 1918.

The 6,000lb Waterloo Boy Model R was considered a
light tractor in 1917, when this photo was taken. It is
shown here with a three-bottom plow.

pose, or general purpose tractors. Not only had Harvester gone into that market, but Case, Oliver, Minneapolis-Moline, Allis-Chalmers, and others were following suit in the late 1920s.

A young engineer had joined Deere in 1911 named Theo Brown. He was a 1901 graduate of Worcester Polytechnic Institute. By 1916, he had risen to be head of the Experimental Department under Chief Engineer Max Sklovsky. In 1923, he was given a seat on the board. Charles Deere Wiman, Director of Manufacturing in 1925, assigned Theo Brown the task of building and testing an all-purpose tractor.

International Harvester began flooding the market with the new Farmall in 1926 (limited

production had started in 1924). It could be used for planting, cultivating, and harvesting, as well as for plowing and driving the thresher. Theo Brown's response was the John Deere Model C, with 10hp at the drawbar and 20hp on the belt.

Because of the success of the Farmall, Deere dealers clamored for the new all-purpose tractor. As a result, field testing and development were somewhat rushed. In 1927 twenty-five Model Cs, were built. Sixteen of these were rebuilt into an improved configuration. Sixty-nine more of this configuration were also, built and sold, but more problems were encountered, so thirty-seven of these were recalled and modified. After 110

The Waterloo Boy Model R, shown here, was in production at the time Deere & Company bought the company.

Production of the R was discontinued after 1918, when it was replaced by the Model N.

Model Cs were built the designation was changed to GP. The designation was changed to better counter the "general purpose" image of the Farmall, and because C sounded too much like the designation of their other tractor, the D. One must remember the quality of the telephone system of the late twenties. The names "Power-farmer" and "Farmrite" were considered but discarded.

The GP was put into production in 1928. It had the same basic layout as the Model D, with wide-spread front wheels. The GP, however, had a high arched front axle that enabled it to straddle the center row and thereby cultivate not two rows, as the Farmall, but three rows at one time. A three-row planter was also developed. The GP was rated for a two-bottom plow.

The GP featured a mechanical implement power lift system, an industry first, and individual rear wheel brakes. It also incorporated a 520rpm power take-off. It, like the Model D, and indeed all John Deere tractors until 1960, used a two-cylinder engine similar to that of the Waterloo Boy.

The interior of the Waterloo Boy engineering department in 1920, after the Deere purchase of that company.

Although the GP continued in the line until 1935, its acceptance by farmers, especially in the South, and its performance in the field, were disappointing. Acceptance was low primarily because of the three-row concept. Farmers wanted two-row equipment in some areas, and four-row in others. Additionally, the $800 price tag was high for a 10/20 Horsepower tractor, with the Farmall selling for around $600.

During the experiments associated with the Model C, one configuration was tried which used a "tricycle" layout; that is, two front wheels close together and the rear wheels on a fifty-inch tread. As soon as it was recognized that the "three-row" layout of the standard GP was not being accepted in all quarters, a tricycle GP was brought out with the above tread arrangement. About twenty-three of these were interspersed in

the GP production during late 1929 and early 1930. Two of these had special rear treads of sixty-eight inches to accommodate two standard potato rows.

Later in 1929, the GPWT, or GP Wide-tread, was introduced. It had longer axles, giving it a seventy-six inch rear tread, allowing it to straddle two regular rows. In addition, some 203 were built with the special "potato" row axles. In 1931, dished wheels were developed, allowing the standard Wide-tread to be convertible to potato rows and the "P" (for potato) series of GPs were eliminated.

The first John Deere orchard tractor was based on the GP. It had fender skirts covering the rear wheels down to below the hubs, and extending over the flywheel and belt pulley. This model, the "GPO," came out in 1930. Some of these

A Waterloo Boy Model R restored by Tony Ridgeway of Ohio. It is pictured at the Two-cylinder Days at the John Deere historic site in Grand Detour, Illinois. The value of such rare antiques is around thirty times the new price of the Model R.

were purchased by the Lindeman Company and were fitted with crawler tracks for use in the large, hilly apple orchards around Yakima, Washington.

The Caterpillar Connection

Deere & Company had started in the harvester business back in 1911. A line of grain binders, corn binders and a corn picker was proving profitable by the late twenties, and the branch houses were pressuring the home office to get into threshing machines and "traveling combined harvesters," also known as combines.

The market for combines looked especially good, as they were being developed more and more for use in the Midwest. After looking into the purchase of available combine designs, a design of their own was produced for the 1928 harvest.

Just as the Deere combine was readied for market, Caterpillar, of Peoria, Illinois, offered to sell Deere their Western Harvester Division, of Stockton, California, with its line of fairly successful combines. The price of 1.25 million dollars was too steep for Deere, and they decided to go it alone.

All went well for Deere, who also bought out the Wagner-Langemo threshing machine line

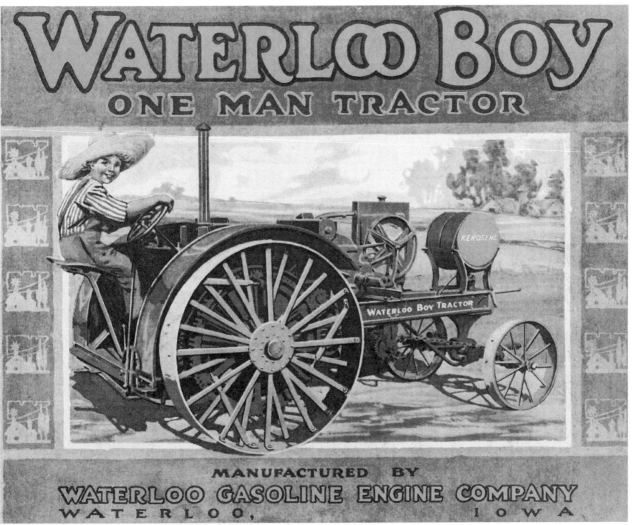

A 1916 showroom poster for the Waterloo Boy Model R featured the cherub-faced boy that became part of the trade mark. The Model R can be readily distinguished from the later Model N by the size of the ring gear inside the rear wheels: it is smaller in diameter on the earlier Model R. Since the later N used a two-speed transmission, the larger final drive gear provided more torque without sacrificing top speed. The R was discontinued in 1918.

in 1929. In 1935, however, Caterpillar was again heard from. Especially in California, the big Cat crawlers were in demand by farmers. Cat dealers had no line of wheeled tractors, and were therefore loosing sales to International Harvester and Allis-Chalmers, who offered both types. Cat purposed a joint dealership arrangement. To sweeten the pot, they also offered to throw in their hillside combine, as well (Deere's several varieties were level-land models). The offer was accepted by Deere, who now also had access to Caterpillar's foreign dealerships. The relationship lasted into the 1960s, but was a diminishing one following World War II as Caterpillar went increasingly into construction and industrial applications.

The Great Depression

William Butterworth had become a nationally recognized individual in his own right and as a business leader. In 1928, he was elected president of the U.S. Chamber of Commerce. As the demands of that office precluded him from day to day operations at Deere, he proposed to the Board that he be elevated to the newly created post of Chairman of the Board, and that Charles

A Waterloo Boy Model N is shown at a demonstration in this 1918 photo. The N is pulling a John Deere Pony double-action disk and a Dunham Culti-packer.

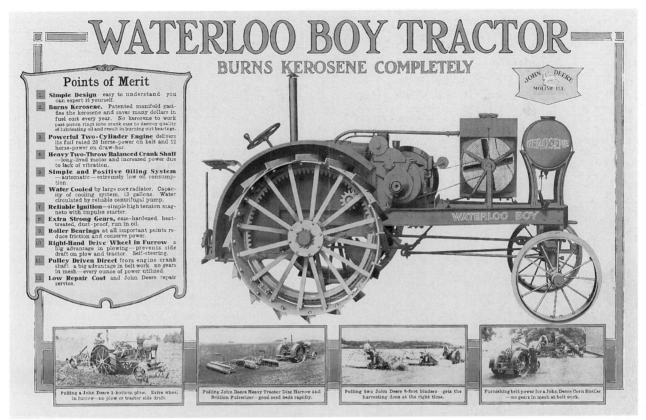

WATERLOO BOY TRACTOR
BURNS KEROSENE COMPLETELY

Points of Merit

1. **Simple Design**—easy to understand you can expect it yourself.
2. **Burns Kerosene.** Patented manifold gasifies the kerosene and saves many dollars in fuel cost every year. No kerosene to work past piston rings into crank case to destroy quality of lubricating oil and result in burning out bearings.
3. **Powerful Two-Cylinder Engine** delivers its full rated 25 horse-power on belt and 12 horse-power on draw-bar.
4. **Heavy Two-Throw Balanced Crank Shaft**—long-lived motor and increased power due to lack of vibration.
5. **Simple and Positive Oiling System**—automatic—extremely low oil consumption.
6. **Water Cooled** by large core radiator. Capacity of cooling system, 13 gallons. Water circulated by reliable centrifugal pump.
7. **Reliable Ignition**—simple high tension magneto with impulse starter.
8. **Extra Strong Gears,** case-hardened, heat-treated, dust-proof, run in oil.
9. **Roller Bearings** at all important points reduce friction and conserve power.
10. **Right-Hand Drive Wheel in Furrow** a big advantage in plowing—prevents side draft on plow and tractor. Self-steering.
11. **Pulley Driven Direct** from engine crank shaft, a big advantage in belt work, no gears in mesh—every ounce of power utilized.
12. **Low Repair Cost** and John Deere repair service.

Pulling a John Deere 3-bottom plow. Drive wheel in furrow—no plow or tractor side draft.

Pulling John Deere Heavy Tractor Disc Harrow and Brillion Pulverizer—good seed beds rapidly.

Pulling two John Deere 8-foot binders—gets the harvesting done at the right time.

Furnishing belt power for a John Deere Corn Sheller—no gears in mesh at belt work.

1920 ad copy for the Waterloo Boy Model N. The N was built from 1918, when Deere bought the company, to 1924, when it was supplanted by the John Deere Model D.

This 1920 photo shows a Waterloo Boy Model N powering a 52in saw. Because of the transverse engine mounting, the belt pulley of the Waterloo Boy was driven directly without gears. This saved power and reduced wear and lubrication problems.

Deere Wiman, great grandson of John Deere, be elected the fourth president of Deere & Company. The Board accepted these proposals, and thus, the family heritage of managing the company was retained.

The early 1930s brought many changes. The coming of the great depression in the fall of 1929 was accompanied by severe drought in the Great Plains. The once prosperous wheat-producing lands were largely abandoned. As the depression spread, farm income dropped worldwide. Tractor sales plummeted. In 1932, tractor sales in the United States dropped to around 19,000 units; the lowest number since 1915. Deere & Company was in much better shape to withstand these times than they were in 1921. Farm prices fell to their lowest point in 1933 and Deere lost over $4 million. In addition, there

was a $4 million reserve set aside for uncollectable debts.

One of the policies the Deere board adopted during these extremely difficult times was that they would not foreclose on their customers, as long as there was any hope of receiving eventual payment. The result was a loyalty to Deere products by the farmers that put the company in good stead for the next several decades.

The Models A and B Tractors

Despite the hard times, Charles Wiman, the new president, believed strongly in product research and development. Although some of the projects had to be curtailed for lack of money, tractor ideas were pursued with vigor. Wiman assigned Theo Brown and his team to come up with two new tractors in the true row-crop, all-

A restored Waterloo Boy Model N performs at the 1994 Waukee, Iowa, antique show. Model N production over-lapped that of the John Deere Model D. This Waterloo Boy sold for about $1,000 in 1920.

purpose tradition. The first, the Model A, was introduced for the 1934 season. The Model B came along a year later.

The year 1934 saw a 40 percent increase in tractor sales over 1933, so industry survivors were optimistic. The new Model A was an instant success. The Model B also filled a substantial need. The Model B was originally available with pneumatic tires, but the A was not available with pneumatic tires until 1935. Each had a four-speed transmission, a PTO, and a belt pulley. The B's engine, a scaled version of the A's, had enough power for one 16in plow, while the A was capable of pulling two fourteens.

These two new GPs had remarkable features that were industry firsts: fully adjustable rear

Many Waterloo Boy tractors were used by municipality and county road crews. This Model N is doing a good job of pulling the converted horse grader (note the buggy seat on the front of the grader). The photo is circa 1920.

wheel widths on splined axles, and hydraulic implement lifts. These alone were enough to insure the success of the A and B. In addition, a single-piece rear axle housing provided more crop clearance and allowed a center location for attachment of the drawbar, as well as a center location for the PTO.

Production of the Models A and B continued through 1952. Almost 300,000 Model As were built, and more than 300,000 Model Bs.

These tractors were immensely profitable for both Deere and the farmers who bought them. Over the years there was a process of continuous up-grade and improvement.

It had developed that the tricycle configuration, with two close-together front wheels, was the conventional arrangement for general purpose machines, rather than the arched wide-front axle of the Deere Model GP. The new tricycle GPs, as As and Bs were called, would vastly out-

A 1920 photo of a Waterloo Boy Model N inside the Waterloo factory. Note the "factory cab."

A horse drawn John Deere-Van Brunt low down press grain drill, circa 1919.

The Dain Manufacturing Company, specialists in haying equipment, became part of Deere & Company in 1910.

This photo, taken in 1920, shows a Dain-John Deere side delivery rake.

Horse drawn walking plows remained a good part of Deere & Company's business through the first half of the twentieth century. Shown here in 1920, a well-matched team seems to be easily handling a Deere steel-beam plow.

sell the standard tread tractors. By 1937, variations with only one front wheel, with adjustable wide-fronts, and extra high-clearance (hi-crop) versions of all front end-types were made available. In addition to these, the Models A and B were available in standard tread versions (called the AR and BR) and in orchard (AO, AOS, and BO) and industrial versions (AI and BI). The

By the beginning of the twentieth century, Deere & Company led the field in cultivator production. This John Deere D9 horse drawn cultivator is working in a potato field in 1920.

BO and BI versions were sent to Lindeman Brothers works in Yakima, Washington, for conversion to crawlers.

Other Developments

In May of 1936, Board Chairman William Butterworth died suddenly. Butterworth had been instrumental in establishing Deere & Company as more than just a family owned business. The business was a family. From upper management to union employees, and even customers, all felt they were a part of the unit. Mr. Butterworth, through his qualities of honesty, thoughtfulness, and concern for others, engendered this tradition that still marks the company today.

During the depression years, other product lines were continued and developed. Among them were stationary engines, haying and harvesting equipment, pickers and planters, tillage equipment, spreaders, elevators, and tractors.

One of the most interesting tractor developments of the times was the baby Deere tractor. By 1936, the Model GP had grown to be the power equal of the Model A and was discontinued. The Model B, too, was growing in power and weight. There was clearly an opening in the lower end of the product line. Accordingly, the engineers at the Deere Wagon Works in Moline were given the go ahead to build their version of a small tractor.

The approach taken by the Moline people was unhampered by the Waterloo traditions. Management dictated a two-cylinder engine, however. The availability of the 8hp Novo engine more or less prompted the configuration. The Novo was essentially the back half of a four-

Ad literature from 1920 shows a horse drawn John Deere wagon.

Baling hay in 1922 with a John Deere-Dain motor press
was a labor-intensive process. It's doubtful this machine
would pass OSHA scrutiny today.

Before Deere & Company acquired Waterloo Boy in 1918, the Waterloo Boy engineers were working on an experimental modern version. Deere product development was quick to get moving with it after the impact of the Ford- son was felt. The experimental Waterloo Boy is shown here 1919 plowing with a three-bottom No. 5 John Deere plow.

cylinder Model A Ford engine. A Ford Model A clutch, three-speed transmission and steering shaft and wheel were also used. The 1,800lb tractor was first called the Model Y. Twenty-four were built, but later recalled.

In the summer of 1937, seventy-eight examples of an improved version, now called the Model 62, were built. The Model 62 used a Hercules engine. Later that year another upgrade resulted in the Model L. Production continued into 1946. More than 12,500 were built.

These capable little tractors (about the size of today's garden tractors) were complete small farm tractors. Specialized equipment included cultivators and single-bottom 12in plows. They were regularly equipped with flat belt pulleys, and were used for driving implements such as shellers and presses. They were unique in the Deere line in that they operated on gasoline, only, and in that they had foot-operated clutches.

A 1922 prototype version of the John Deere Model D. Note the similarity to the experimental Waterloo Boy.

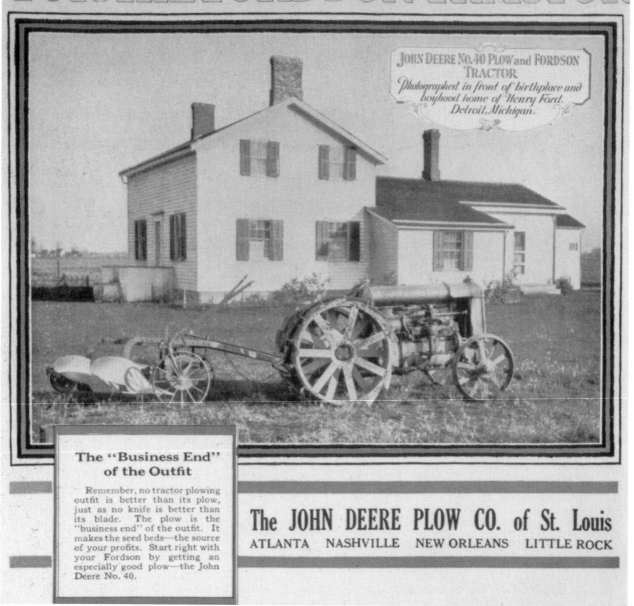

JOHN DEERE IMPLEMENTS FOR THE FORDSON TRACTOR

JOHN DEERE No. 40 PLOW and FORDSON TRACTOR
Photographed in front of birthplace and boyhood home of Henry Ford, Detroit, Michigan.

The "Business End" of the Outfit

Remember, no tractor plowing outfit is better than its plow, just as no knife is better than its blade. The plow is the "business end" of the outfit. It makes the seed beds—the source of your profits. Start right with your Fordson by getting an especially good plow—the John Deere No. 40.

The JOHN DEERE PLOW CO. of St. Louis
ATLANTA   NASHVILLE   NEW ORLEANS   LITTLE ROCK

The Fordson decimated the sales of Waterloo Boy tractors in 1922 when Henry Ford dropped the price for a Fordson to $395. In addition to accelerating their work on the new Model D tractor, Deere engineers built the No. 40 plow especially for the Fordson. Ford made no implements for the tractor. Shown here is 1923 ad copy featuring the Fordson.

A Fordson tractor drives a John Deere No. 5 sheller in this 1926 photo. The Fordson was a 20hp belt 10hp drawbar tractor which sold for about half the price of the John Deere Model D. Ford sold ten times as many tractors as Deere sold Model Ds during the ten years that the Fordson was built in the U.S. The lightweight, powerful, and inexpensive Fordson influenced the designs of all competitors. The Fordson shown here could not have been much more than a year old when the photo was taken; notice the deteriorated quality of the paint.

A 1924 photo showing the interior of the John Deere Waterloo tractor works. Notice the lack of electricity and the dirt floor.

Another inside view of the Waterloo factory in 1924. Over the man's head, an electric motor is powering the line shaft.

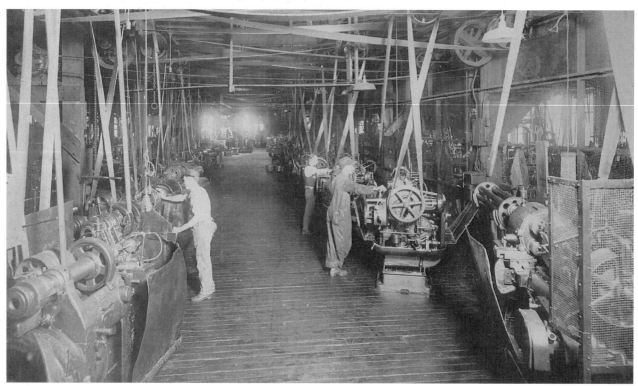

In this 1924 view of the Waterloo factory, a few electric lights are visible.

A 1926 photo shows a pair of mule-drawn John Deere riding cultivators working in a corn field.

JOHN DEERE FARM TRACTOR
MODEL D 15-27

THE SIMPLE TRACTOR THAT IS LIGHT IN WEIGHT AND SMALL IN DIMENSIONS, BUT BIG IN POWER

Ad literature for the 1925 Model D tractor. The first fifty Model Ds built in 1923 had 26in spoked flywheels and a direct steering rod on the left side. The next 820, or so, had the 26in flywheel, but a jointed steering rod. In late 1924, a 24in spoked flywheel was substituted. From 1926 on, a solid flywheel was used.

This restored 1925 John Deere Model D, with the 24in spoked flywheel is owned by John Davis of Maplewood, Ohio.

Men in the John Deere Harvester Works making wheels in 1924.

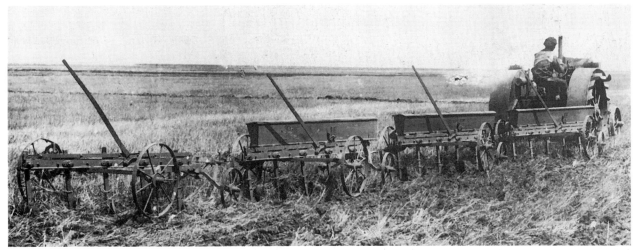

During the lean years of 1922 and 1923 a number of Waterloo Boys were sold to Russia. This photo shows one pulling a series of implements called bookers.

Model D tractors coming off the Waterloo Works assembly line in 1924. The influence of the Fordson's mass production prompted rethinking of assembly methods.

A 1924 John Deere Model D pulling a binder and a Kellogg shocker.

In this 1926 photo, a prototype combine shown equipped to pull the grain wagon along side. The combine is pow-ered by a four-cylinder engine and a Model D tractor is pulling the outfit.

A Model D, with hard rubber tires, pulls a road scraper in a field demonstration near Lincoln, Nebraska, February 13, 1926.

A John Deere portable grain elevator is shown in this 1927 photo, as well as a John Deere No. 255 "horsepower" drive.

A studio photo of the Model C taken in 1928. In 1926 Deere decided to develop a tractor smaller than the Model D. The result was the Model C, which came out in March of 1927. By late 1928, most of the 110 Model Cs delivered were recalled and rebuilt as the Model GP, which stood for "General Purpose," that is, the tractor had a rear power take-off as well as a belt pulley, and was designed for use with mounted cultivators as well as pulled implements. The introduction of the International Harvester "Farmall" in 1924 caused a great deal of interest in the concept by row-crop farmers. The GP was produced from 1928 through 1935.

A John Deere Model GP tractor pulls two sickle-bar mowers that were designed to be pulled by horses. Rigs to adapt these, and other horse implements to tractors were common in 1928 when this picture was taken.

A 1928 Model C tractor plows with a No. 40C plow. The No. 40 was a conventional 2-14 plow, and was developed for the popular Fordson in the early 1920s, but later adapted as the 40C for the John Deere Model C tractor.

Purported to be a Model C by the archive photo data, this tractor is pulling a No. 3 corn picker in this 1928 photo. The tractor must, therefore, be less than a year old; certainly less than two. The dull paint on the tractor is a far cry from the high-gloss finishes applied by today's collectors. Notice the fine pair of mules pulling the wagon. Today's generation has no idea of the amount of work a team like that could do day in and day out.

A Model GP powers a Letz grinder via the flat belt pulley.
The photo was taken in 1928.

The venerable Model D with a No. 2 two bottom two-way plow. Notice how the tall weeds are being covered. The D was the favorite plowing tractor by many farmers. This photo was taken in 1928.

A 1929 photo of the Syracuse John Deere Plow Works.

A John Deere Model D tractor with a No. 2 combine harvesting Kansas wheat, circa 1929.

A Model GPWT (GP Wide-Tread) with a No. 400 cotton and corn planter. The GPWT version emerged in 1929 to counter objections of farmers who did not like the three-row concept (with the tractor straddling the center row). The Wide-tread had longer rear axles (76in tread) for straddling two rows and a narrow front. The GPWT remained in production, along with the regular GP until 1935.

A 1929 Model D John Deere pulls a converted horse-drawn disk and a Van Brunt grain drill. Note how the driver's position is convenient for manually adjusting the trailed implements.

Two collie dogs wonder about the Model GP tractor going back and forth operating the No. 2 hay stacker. Stacking loose hay for outside storage was an art form in 1929 when this photo was taken.

Threshing in 1930 was a labor intensive operation, although in this scene, four men are leaning on the Model D tractor (probably enjoying the sound). Bundles are being fed into the thresher from both sides, indicating ample power is coming from the D. The thresherman, bent over atop the rig, is checking the tailings elevator to see how much grain is being recycled. Note the fly covers on the horses; motion of the strings tended to keep the flies from irritating the horses. The thresher is a Grain Saver, John Deere's first model.

August 1930, a John Deere tractor binder with remote controls for the Model D tractor, allows one man to perform the harvest.

DEERE & CO.
MOLINE, ILL.

ESTABLISHED 1847

LEADING IN 1897

50 YEARS OF PROGRESS. ★

Deere & Company began using the deer in their advertising in about 1875. By 1897, it looked more like an elk than a deer. This painting was for a calendar celebrating fifty years in Moline, Illinois. The Moline business actually began in 1848, but according to Robert Tate, John Deere's partner, Deere himself, made the mistake of bricking the wrong year into the new building. The mistake was never rectified. The company now claims the 1837 date when the blacksmith shop was founded, so the point is moot. *Deere Archives*

Another piece of calendar art, from the year 1899. The deer is even more elk-like than it had been before. *Deere Archives*

A calendar picture from 1924, entitled "Aces All" shows an early Model D tractor pulling a No. 5 plow. This art was intended to equate the tractor with air transportation, both being products of the modern age. *Deere Archives*

A very early Waterloo Boy Model R (Style G) of 1916 vintage. This one has the radiator on the right and a smaller fuel tank than was used on later models. The protrusion in front of the right rear wheel is the receptacle for the starting crank. The small tank on the inside of the left fender (there was one on the right, too, not visible here), was for oil for the drive gear mesh. Gasoline was carried in the right end of the fuel tank for starting. The main part of the tank is for kerosene. *Deere Archives*

The Model N Waterloo Boy was built from 1917 to 1924. It can be distinguished from the earlier Model R by the size of the ring gear inside the rear wheel. For the Model N, it is nearly as large as the wheel itself; on the Model R, this gear is noticeably smaller. The example shown was built in 1920 and is owned by Don Wolf of Ft. Wayne, Indiana. *Andrew Morland*

This 1930 John Deere Model GP was restored by Kent Koester of K&K Restorations. It is owned by Don Wolf, a retired Ft. Wayne, Indiana, businessman. The 1930 model had a 339ci two-cylinder side-valve engine. Maximum belt horsepower was twenty-four. *Andrew Morland*

The John Deere Model GP was introduced in 1928 and was the second production tractor, not including the Dain, to bear the name John Deere. Production continued through 1935. The GP began life as the Model C, but this was soon changed to reflect the growing interest by customers in the all-purpose, or General Purpose, concept in tractors. Shown here is a later year model GP. To be correct, the leaping deer picture should be between the words John and Deere. *Robert N. Pripps*

A 1935 John Deere Model D. The 1935 model had a three-speed transmission, replacing the two-speed unit used previously. This one, owned by Don Wolf, has cut-off steel wheels with 8-28 rear tires and 7.50-18 fronts. Old timers say they would rather plow with a Model D than with any other tractor. *Andrew Morland*

This rare 1935 John Deere Model BR has the earlier 149ci engine. After 1938, the engines were 175ci. The BR was rated at 14.25 belt horsepower with the smaller engine and 17.5 with the larger. Master Case collector John Davis, of Maplewood, Ohio, owns this beauty. *Andrew Morland*

The John Deere AOS was a Model AO (Orchard) tractor with streamlined sheet metal to allow the machine to slip through the branches. Fewer than 900 were built between 1936 and 1940. Shown here is Neil West's 1937 AOS. West is from Bettendorf, Iowa. *Robert N. Pripps*

This rare John Deere Model BNH was one of only sixty-five built. It is owned by Bruce Johnson of Lily Lake, Illinois. Johnson, a consummate restorer of unstyled Model B tractors, has had his work displayed at every Two-cylinder Club Expo. Johnson's BNH is a 1938 model. *Robert N. Pripps*

This impeccably restored BO Lindeman Crawler is owned by Bruce Johnson of Lily Lake, Illinois. It is one of ten unstyled John Deere Model B tractors owned and restored by Johnson. The Lindeman is shown at the Two-cylinder Days event at the John Deere homestead in Grand Detour, Illinois. *Robert N. Pripps*

This nicely-restored John Deere Model GW was seen at the 1994 Two-cylinder Days event at the John Deere homestead. The big Model G was normally equipped with the tricycle front end. The Adjustable wide-front, as shown here, was quite rare and only available between 1947 and 1953. *Robert N. Pripps*

By 1949, when this John Deere AWH was built, the engine displacement had been increased from 309ci to 321ci. After 1947, a molded pressed steel frame replaced the angle iron frame used before. The AWH was wide and high; it had an adjustable wide front end, and longer king pin struts. The rear tires were 12.4x42, thereby raising the rear end higher than with the standard 11x38 tires. This AWH is owned by Lyle Pals of Egan, Illinois. *Andrew Morland*

This 1950 John Deere Model AR is owned by Jon Davis of Maplewood, Ohio. He got it from his grandfather, who was the original owner. Until 1949, the Model AR was un-styled. They were among the last to receive the Dreyfuss styling treatment. *Andrew Morland*

The John Deere Model 40 was the first upgrade of the Model M and was built between 1953 and 1956. It was available with either a gasoline engine or an all-fuel engine (designed to use distillate or gasoline). Approximately 33,000 of the 2,750lb Model 40 were built. Shown here is a 1953 Model 40S (Standard), with an orchard muffler, owned by Bob Jensen of Montgomery, Illinois. *Robert N. Pripps*

The Model 40 was introduced in 1953 in 40S Standard, 40T convertible Tricycle or wide-front and 40C Crawler versions. Like the Model M, which the 40 replaced, it was built in Dubuque, Iowa. It featured a three-point hitch with live hydraulics. This Model 40T (Widefront) looks particularly nice in its Highway Yellow paint. It is owned by Larry Goodwin, Genesco, Illinois. *Robert N. Pripps*

A 1956 photo shows a John Deere No. 400 hay cuber harvester with a No. 75 Hi-Dump wagon. Hay cubing, or pelletizing, was popular in the southwest in the seventies. It was an effort it make hay a higher-density commodity for transportation. *Deere Archives*

The Model 420 replaced the Model 40 in 1956. The 420 incorporated the load compensating Powr-Trol implement hitch. It was available in six versions including the T, or convertible, configuration shown here. *Robert N. Pripps*

The Model 60 replaced the Model A in 1953 and represented a substantial upgrade. The 60-O (Orchard), however was basically the same as the AO, but with a new grill. This extremely rare LPG version was only built in 1956 and 1957. *Robert N. Pripps*

Shown is Don Wolf's nicely restored 1959 Model 430W (gasoline). The 430 was available in seven configurations, including the row-crop utility type shown here (designat-ed by the W). Also available were the Standard (S), the Utility (U), the Hi-crop (H), the Special (V), the tricycle, or convertible (T), and the Crawler (C). *Andrew Morland*

Orv Rothgarn's Model 730 (gasoline) is one of more than twenty John Deere tractors in his Owatonna, Minnesota, collection. He also has more than 300 toy, or model trac-tors. *Andrew Morland*

This Model 830 Rice Special tractor's profile is dominated by the huge tires on the rear. The 830 was the ultimate in John Deere standard tread tractors and was rated for six plow bottoms or a twenty-foot disk. The 830 was only available with a diesel engine, but the buyer had the option of a V-4 starting motor or a 24-Volt electric starter. This 1959 Model 830 Rice Special is owned by Raymond Armistead, Adairville, Kentucky. *Robert N. Pripps*

The Titan combines were introduced in 1979. Shown is the popular mid-sized 7720 Titan II. This one is equipped with the optional hydrostatic rear wheel drive. *Deere Archives*

The Model 4230 was a Waterloo-built medium-size tractor of 100hp. It used the six-cylinder 404ci diesel or gasoline engine. The gasoline version was discontinued after 1972, however. The shine on the moldboards of the three-bottom two-way plow would have made John Deere proud. *Deere Archives*

Mannheim-built tractors for sale in the U.S. differed from those for European use. Note the front-mounted headlights, front fenders, and rear fender-mounted ROPS on this four-cylinder Model 2140 for Europe. *Deere Archives*

The Model 4850 replaced the 4840 in 1983. This Waterloo-built favorite offered increased power from 466ci turbocharged and aftercooled diesel. Power was 193 PTO horsepower. *Deere Archives*

The 2750 was a Mannheim-built tractor of 75hp, built between 1983 and 1986. It is shown here in the low-profile Orchard version pulling a mounted chisel plow. Improvements over the previous 2640, which it replaced, were faster-acting hydraulics and better connections for remote cylinders plus 5hp more. *Deere Archives*

Introduced in 1988 as a special purpose model, this 2955 John Deere tractor has a 96in wide front axle. It is shown with an S-tine field cultivator next to a field of ripening tobacco. This Mannheim-built tractor used a 359ci six-cylinder engine. It featured twelve forward speeds, including those provided by the partial-range power shift. The tractor was rated at 85 PTO horsepower and had a basic weight of about 10,000lb. *Deere Archives*

A favorite with the highway departments, the 2355, was brought out in 1987 and replaced the 2350. Engine improvements in this Mannheim tractor resulted in improved fuel economy. The four-cylinder engine yielded 56hp. It is shown with a box scraper. *Deere Archives*

The Model 8640 was built from 1979 to 1982 (replacing the 8630). Most of the improvements of this new model were internal. These included new, stronger, and quieter transmission and final-drive gears, increased lift capacity, front and rear differential locks, and stronger engine components. A computerized monitoring system, called the Investigator, warned of malfunctions. Several improvements provided a smoother ride for the operator; a welcome change because of the long hours of use these machines got per day. *Deere Archives*

A 36hp Model 920 works Canadian soil with three-bottom F-45 mounted plow. The 920 was a Mannheim-built tractor. *Deere Archives*

JOHN DEERE General Purpose Wide-Tread Tractor

The Row-Crop Tractor that does ALL FARM JOBS within Its Power Range

— One-Man Operated.

— Complete 2- or 4-Row Equipment.

Has the John Deere Power Lift — saves the hard work of raising and lowering equipment by hand. SPEEDS UP THE WORK.

GET ALL the FACTS About This Tractor That's Built to Meet Your Requirements.

This 1930 ad copy touts the John Deere GPWT tractor. The GP tractor came in many forms but all had chain-driven rear wheels, as did the Model D.

A farmer's first tractor will always be remembered with pride. It shows on the face of this man giving his boy a ride on the fender of his GP, circa 1930.

A GP tractor pulling a No. 5A combine in 1934. The No. 5 replaced the No. 1 in 1929. The No. 5A replaced the No. 5 in 1934. These combines were all powered by four-cylinder engines.

Many farmers opted for the threshing machine instead of the combine even after World War II. Shown here in 1935 is a John Deere Model D powering a big 28in x 50in John Deere thresher. In 1929 Deere & Company bought the Wagner-Langemo Company, a thresher manufacturer.

A scene from December 1935, near Reese, Michigan. A Model B, two Model Ds, and a Model GP plow, while a Model A pulls a harrow.

A 1936 Model DI (Industrial) tractor pulls a Caterpillar grader. Only about 100 industrial versions of the D were made. Model Ds built after 1931 had intake and exhaust pipes extending well above the hood.

John Deere No. 4 Enclosed-Gear Mower

WHEN you pull into the field for the first time with the John Deere No. 4 Enclosed-Gear Mower, there's a real surprise awaiting you. One trip around the field will convince you that you've never seen a mower that can "hold a candle to it". Its good work in all field and crop conditions, its smooth, quiet running, its light draft, and its convenience and ease of operation put it in a class by itself.

Enclosed gears running in oil; heavy, one-piece axle with no holes to weaken it; simple, balanced, two-step gears; high-grade roller and ball bearings; "differential" pawl plates at ends of axle where they are easy to inspect; high, easy foot and hand lifts; durable, smooth-running clutch; accurately-fitted, long-lived cutting parts; and simple adjustments for re-aligning cutter bar and recentering knife are but a few of the features which contribute to its greater satisfaction down through the years.

You can get the John Deere in 4-1/2-, 5-, 6- and 7-foot sizes with a wide variety of equipment to meet your particular needs.

Plan to own a John Deere No. 4 Enclosed-Gear Mower before the next haying season begins. Your John Deere dealer will be glad to point out its many valuable advantages.

The John Deere No. 4 Mower equipped with quick-turn tongue truck.

1935 ad literature for the John Deere No. 4 mower.

Six experimental versions of a new row-crop tractor were built in 1933 designated "AA." Shown here is one of them, complete with a hydraulically lifted cultivator. These tractors were the prototypes of the Model A, which was introduced in 1934.

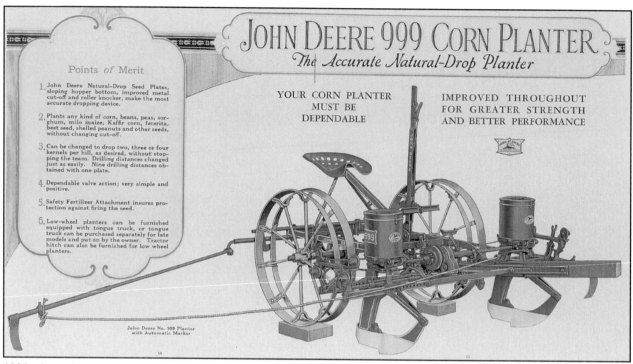

1935 advertising material for the 999 corn planter.

The Model B tractor came out in 1935, a year after the Model A. Here is one of the earliest versions (note the four-bolt pedestal) pulling a No. 10 corn picker near Dell Rapids, South Dakota.

Next page
"You'll do better work and more work . . .," is the pitch of this 1936 farm magazine ad.

Reduce Tillage Costs With This Equipment

The John Deer-Van Brunt Model CC Cultivator is great for handling cover crops. Wheels inside frame do not interfere. Shields protect foliage.

John Deere Model HD Heavy-Duty Disk Harrow, latest in tractor-controlled disk harrows, has no superior in orchard or grove work.

John Deer Model OF Offset Disk Harrow is a great favorite especially in California and the Pacific northwest; low-down and rugged. Offsets right or left.

YOU'LL do better work and more work, reduce production costs and increase crop yields with the aid of this dependable, easy-handling, tractor-controlled John Deere tillage equipment—rugged disk harrows, spring- and stiff-tooth cultivators, and spring-tooth harrows—designed to meet all requirements in orchard, grove, vineyard and field.

No job comes too tough for these machines—they're built from the ground up to take the hard knocks.

* * *

The Model CC Cultivator can be furnished with shovels in various styles and sizes for all tillage—making seed beds, cultivating orchards, alfalfa, stubble land, and eradicating all weeds. Simple adjustment for deep or shallow tillage. Screw depth regulator operated from tractor. Power lift raises teeth when you pull a rope. Shields protect foliage.

* * *

Front and rear gangs of the disk harrows are angled and straightened independently by tractor power—just pull a trip rope. Heavy steel welded construction, heat-treated steel blades, Alemite lubrication, heavy-duty chilled bearings, adjustable spring pressure, wide spacing of disks—these are features that assure good work, long life and low upkeep.

* * *

Teeth of the John Deere tractor-controlled spring-tooth harrow are raised and lowered in an entirely new, simple manner, from the tractor seat. No long levers to catch on low-hanging limbs. The combination of John Deere *special-process* heat-treated teeth and *heat-treated* tooth bars gives you heavy duty construction that means years of good work in orchard and field.

In orchard or in field, the John Deere Tractor-controlled Spring-Tooth Harrow saves time in cultivation and in weeding.

JOHN DEERE

The deal made with Caterpillar in 1936 gave Deere the great No. 36 Combine. The No. 36 was originally designed by Holt. The name was changed to Caterpillar in 1929 when Holt and Best, giants of the crawler tractor industry, merged. Even though the No. 36 had its own engine, it still required twelve horses to pull it.

Deere & Company President, Charles Wiman, poses with a No. 52 plow in 1936.

"Oh Lord, the field is so big and my plow is so small." A
Model B tractor pulls a 14in one bottom No. 51 plow near
Trent, South Dakota, circa 1936.

A Model AI (Industrial) tractor with loader fills a 1929 Model A Ford dump truck. The AI was built from 1936 to 1941 and was the industrial version of the standard-tread Model AR.

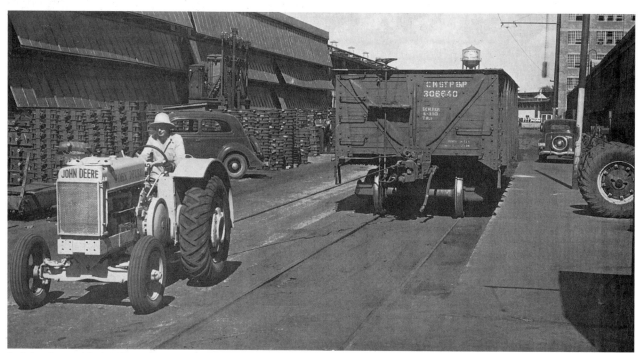

A John Deere Model AI pulls a rail car at the Deere plant in 1936. The industrial version of the Model A had special mounting pads on the frame for industrial equipment such as sweepers and loaders. Railroad buffs will notice the rail car is from the Chicago-Milwaukee-St. Paul & Pacific Railroad.

In 1937, cultivating was one of the biggest tractor jobs for the corn farmer. The Model A tractor with a A492 mounted cultivator was just about the best rig for the job. This one, seen near Wellington, Illinois, seems to have a revised seat.

There were industrial versions of the Model B, as well as the Model A. Shown here is a Model BI with a mower doing county highway department duty in 1938. The BI was built from 1936 to 1941.

A rare antique such as this 1938 John Deere ANH demands a perfect restoration. Only twenty-six ANHs were made. It is owned by the Keller Family of Forest Junction, Wisconsin. It has a four-speed transmission and a 309ci engine. Deere built the Model A from 1934 to 1952. The ANH version had a single front wheel and was higher than the standard Model A. *Andrew Morland*

A rare restored BNH appeared at the Freeport, Illinois, show in 1994.

The AR was the standard-tread version of the Model A. This nicely restored AR has triple-wide rear wheels. Unstyled ARs were built from 1935 to 1940.

This restored John Deere Model B has the optional round-top fenders. It was seen at the 1994 Waukee, Iowa, show.

This unstyled John Deere Model A has the early decal type on the side of the hood. The "leaping deer" and the script-like G and P were not used on hoods after 1935.

The difference between early and late hood decals can be seen in the photo of restored tractors at the 1994 Waukee, Iowa, show. The AN in the foreground has the latter type, while the A in the background has the earlier type with the leaping deer.

The Model G was introduced in 1938 as a full three-plow big brother to the Models A and B. A 1938 model is shown here with a potato planter near Eldridge, New York.

March 1938, near Phoenix, Arizona. A Model BN culti-
vates beets with a mounted beet and bean cultivator.

The Lindeman Power Equipment Company of Yakima, Washington, converted just under 2,000 John Deere Model BO tractors to crawler tracks between 1939 and 1948. Beginning with the earlier GPO tractor, Lindeman purchased partially finished tractors from the Waterloo Works. They added steering clutches, controls, and the tracks. The little crawlers proved to be just what orchard farmers of the west needed. Deere purchased Lindeman in 1946, and together, they continued to make crawler versions of the M, 40, 420, 430, and 440. Deere eventually moved the operation to Dubuque, Iowa. Crawler production is still a big part of Deere's industrial equipment base.

An unstyled Model B, with round-top fenders, and the old closed-tread Firestone rear tires, works with a Van Brunt CC cultivator near Waterloo, Iowa, in May of 1939. The CC spring-tine cultivator was introduced in the early thirties and stayed in the line into the fifties.

After the Models A and B, the D was the next tractor to receive the Henry Dreyfuss styling treatment. 1939 Model Ds, such as the one shown here, and on through 1953, were styled. This one is working with a PTO rice binder near Stuttgart, Arizona.

This 1941 photo, taken near Genesco, Illinois, shows hay baling using a PTO version of the old Dain-John Deere baler. The tractor is a Model G. Note the French and Hecht wheel weights.

A Model B with a slant dash. The slant dash held three instruments: oil pressure, water temperature, and amperes. The slant dash was used from 1939 until 1946, when an electrical system was installed.

Fewer than 900 of these Model AOS tractors were built between 1936 and 1940. "AOS" stood for Model A, Orchard, Streamlined.

This unstyled Model L, owned by Harold Dobbratz, is a 1937 version. The Model L was about a 10hp tractor and was sold from 1937 to 1946.

An unusual John Deere cable-driven manure loader is shown here attached to an unstyled Model B. Such loaders were in Deere's inventory in 1939 and 1940.

A rare John Deere Model 62, forerunner of the Model L, is owned by Don Klein. It is one of only twenty-two still in existence. The JD logo below the radiator was used on the pre-production models.

A Model G plows with a No. 93 disk plow.

A Model L shells corn with a No. 4 Corn Sheller at the
John Deere experimental farm near Moline, Illinois.

The importance of horse (and mule)-drawn implements was not overlooked by Deere even in the late thirties— many farmers still used them. Shown here is a 999 wire-trip planter and a spring-tooth harrow.

A one-row horse-drawn potato planter working near Syracuse, New York. The photo was taken in 1937.

Bunky Meese, of Freeport, Illinois, owns this 1938 Model G tractor. It is one of the first 4250 Model Gs, known as low-radiator Gs. Radiator size was increased after that to overcome cooling shortcomings.

Chapter 5

Modern Equipment:
1938-1962

"Happy days are here again
The skies above are blue again."
Theme song of the New Deal

Bigger Row-crops

With the farm and labor legislation of 1938, the worst of the depression was over. Farmers with large acreages were beginning to prosper; so were the implement manufacturers. International Harvester was still in first place by a wide margin, with Deere second. Case, Oliver, Massey, Allis-Chalmers, and Minneapolis rounded out the competition.

Harvester had introduced the three-plow F-30 Farmall in 1931. It had enjoyed its solitary place in the over-20 drawbar horsepower row-

An early-styled Model B tractor is shown here in 1939 pulling a new five-foot No. 11 combine. Model B tractors are referred to as "early-styled" between 1938 and 1946 and "late-styled" from 1947 through 1952. The No. 11 combine had a unique right-hand cutter bar. The No. 11-A came out in 1940 with a more conventional left-hand cutter.

crop class for nearly eight years. Deere engineers had their hands full with the new Models A, B, and L, and in keeping the Model D current. The Model GP was dropped in 1935.

By 1936, rumors abounded that other companies were entering the over-20 drawbar horsepower row-crop tractor class. Theo Brown and company began working on a tractor they called the Model F, thus completing the letter sequence from A to F (the Model C was redesignated the GP, and the Model E designation was used for stationary engines). It wasn't long before management intervened, reasoning the Harvester had usurped the letter F with their line (F-12, F-20,

and F-30). So, the letter F was skipped and G selected.

The compromise in tractor design has always been between power and fuel consumption. Deere engineers wanted enough power to pull three plows, for 25in to 30in threshing machines, and for the new PTO combines. Yet they wanted fuel consumption to be like that of the highly successful Model D (also a three-plow machine) or the competing Farmall. Eventually, a 412.5ci two-cylinder engine was selected giving the G a drawbar horsepower continuous rating of 20.7 in official testing at the University of Nebraska (the maximum drawbar horsepower was

Henry Dreyfuss applied his artistic styling genius to John Deere Models A and B tractors for 1938. By the 1930s, people in all walks of life recognized that well engineered products also looked good. This Model B is shown with a Dain push-rake.

34.5). The F-30 was rated at 20.9 drawbar horsepower.

The Model G was ready for the 1938 crop season. Besides the G and F-30, the field now also included the Oliver Row Crop 80 (23.3 drawbar horsepower) and the Massey-Harris 101R (24.8 drawbar horsepower).

Not long after its introduction, Deere began receiving complaints about the G overheating, especially from farmers in warmer climates.

The John Deere Model D received the Dreyfuss styling treatment in 1939 as shown in this slightly air brushed photo from 1940. It is shown pulling a new No. 21 two- row corn picker. The No. 21 replaced the No. 20, which had been in the inventory since 1929.

A styled John Deere Model D shows one of the reasons for its popularity over the years; a comfortable stand-up platform. This Model D is pulling a damming lister.

Deere finally concluded the radiator size was in error and after Serial Number 4251, the height of the radiator was increased. Those prior to that serial are now known as "Low-radiator Gs." The taller radiator interfered with the overhead steering shaft, so this radiator had a notch in the cast upper tank, which allowed passage of the shaft.

Henry Dreyfuss

By 1935, durable goods companies were employing styling and product differentiation to improve sales. Cars, for example, had been quite a bit alike: boxy, four-cylinder engines, clam fenders, exposed radiators. By the mid-1030s, styling had become individualistic. Six, eight, twelve, and even sixteen cylinder engines had replaced the fours, and radiator grills were the hallmark of styling.

While there had been some attempts at dressing up tractors, no real "form and function" styling had been done until the new Oliver Hart-Parr 70 was brought out in 1935. It immediately

The Model D was a favorite with the rice producers over its thirty-year history. A 1939 styled Model D is shown in Bowdre, Mississippi, pulling a No. 53 rice plow.

overshadowed the competition and it influenced tractor design from then on. It was functional, styled, equipped with a starter and lights, and had an instrument panel and finger-tip controls just like a car. Advertising of the day showed "Sister" and "Bud" taking their turns at the wheel. And it sold, making big inroads into the market for the John Deere Models A and B.

The Oliver Hart-Parr 70 marked one of the most profound turning points in the farm implement industry's history. It reflected both the optimism of the improving economic situation and the increasing influence of the automobile on tractor design. Deere engineers looked at their wares in relation to the Oliver. Theirs looked old fashioned.

One of the most respected industrial designers of the time was Henry Dreyfuss of New York

A 1939 Model B tractor is shown here near Valparaiso, Indiana, pulling a No. 52 plow. This tractor does not have the hydraulic lift system.

A styled Model A tractor is shown in this 1939 photo pulling and powering a Dain hay press baler. The baler still required two men riding on the machine to insert the wires.

City. He had been involved in improving the looks and sales of products from telephones to kitchen appliances. The Deere engineers pressured Charles Stone, then head of manufacturing, to engage Dreyfuss to style their tractors. When the board also began pressing Stone to do something about styling, he relented, and dispatched an engineer to talk to Dreyfuss. The fanciful story is that the Deere engineer arrived at Dreyfuss' office unannounced, in the fall of 1937, wearing a straw hat and fur coat. This so impressed the famed designer with the potential for tractor redesign, that he left for Waterloo that same day.

The first tractors attacked by Dreyfuss were the Models A and B. The striking new sheet metal and ergonomics redesign were ready for the 1938 model year and were an overwhelming

An early-styled Model B pulling a No. B241 middlebreaker plow. The tires are so new that the molding beads are still visible. Between 1938 and 1946 Model Bs had a 175ci two-cylinder engine. The engine produced about 18hp on the belt on kerosene fuel.

success. Other new models were styled along the same lines. As time permitted, almost all the other tractors and implements received the Dreyfuss touch, reflecting ruggedness and strength. Deere and Dreyfuss formed an association that has lasted, influencing current designs of Deere products. Tractors with the Dreyfuss touch are known as "styled;" those without are considered "unstyled."

Smaller Row-crops

Tractors, like people, gain weight with age, or so it seems. The Model B was instituted as the low end of the row-crop scale in 1935. By 1939, its weight had gone up from 3,300lb to 4,550lb. Drawbar horsepower had gone from less than twelve to over eighteen. International Harvester was enjoying a free hand in the truck garden market with their 12 drawbar horsepower F-14. Deere did have the Model L and the newly upgraded, but similar, Model LA in that category, but these were not a true row-crops, and sales were somewhat disappointing.

In September of 1938, the Deere board issued a decision to make a one-plow tractor, called the Model H and styled like the Models A

The John Deere Wagon Works in Moline built the Model L small tractor from 1937 through 1946. It was the first John Deere with a vertical two-cylinder engine and a foot clutch. In 1941 the L was joined by the Model LA, which was a little more powerful. The Model L, as shown in this 1939 photo, received the Dreyfuss styling treatment during the 1938 model year. This Model L is shown operating a home-made cord wood saw.

The Model H was the Waterloo Works answer to the requirement for a small, inexpensive tractor in the true John Deere tradition. When it came on the scene in 1939 it looked for all the world like a scale model of the Models A and B. Shown at the John Deere Historic Site in Grand Detour is a well-restored and rare Model HWH. The HWH is a Model H with a wide front end and the high-crop configuration.

and B. It was to be ready for the 1939 season. The traditional two-cylinder engine would be used, but it would be a mere 99.7ci. Available in January 1939, the tractor was rated at 10 drawbar horsepower and weighed about 3,000lb. Its price, in 1939, was $650. With such a low price, farmers reluctant to spend the money to replace their horse team now had no excuse. The market garden farmers also found the Model H to be "just the ticket." Finally, large acreage farmers found the H to be the ideal chore tractor, sparing their big machines for serious work. Over 60,000 were sold in the next eight years of production.

The Lindeman Crawler

In 1930, as the grip of the depression tightened, Lindeman Brothers of Yakima, Washington, acquired a John Deere dealership. Many of their customers were apple growers, and neither of the two John Deere models, the D and the GP, were well suited for orchard work. They were too high to fit under the branches, and had too many upward protrusions. The brothers be-

This Model H is owned by and was restored by master tractor collector-restorer John Eggers of Two Rivers, Wisconsin.

gan to manufacture some cultivation tools that had extension drawbars, so that they would run out to the side of the tractor and get closer to the tree trunk.

Next the Lindeman Brothers took a standard tread GP and modified it with special axle castings to lower it. They also lowered the seat and cleaned up the things sticking out of the hood. The folks at Deere were impressed. The Lindeman's ideas were adopted and John Deere's first orchard tractor was born; the GPO.

In 1932, the Brothers again notified John Deere that they had something to show them. They had installed the tracks from a Best Thirty crawler on a John Deere D. They eventually constructed three of these, which were thoroughly tested by both Lindeman and Deere. The outcome was the decision to drop the idea for the D, but to apply it to the GPO. Lindeman purchased partially finished orchard tractors from Deere and installed a conventional crawler running gear.

A Model H is shown in this 1940 photo pulling a No. 596 side delivery rake. The rather unusual tire on the rake would present a challenge for the restorer to replace today.

It wasn't long before Deere announced that the GP was being replaced by the Model B. An orchard version of standard tread B, the BO, would be offered. The Lindemans immediately began adding tracks.

The Lindeman Crawlers, as they came to be known, were just right for the hilly apple orchards in Washington and Oregon. The low stance, freedom from protrusions above the hood and the hillside stability made the Lindemans good sellers. They also found good usage in flat land farming in the West. Approximately 2,000

BO Lindeman crawlers were sold between 1939 and 1947, when the Model BO was discontinued. Deere purchased the Lindeman company in 1946, continuing to make crawler versions of its small tractors through 1960s.

The Three-Point Hitch

Oliver had gotten the jump on the competition in 1935 with the introduction of their Model 70. Things changed by 1939, however. Both John Deere and International Harvester had retained the services of world-renowned stylists;

The John Deere-Van Brunt grain drill had been in the catalog since the twenties with only minimal changes when this photo was taken in 1941. The tractor is a styled Model B.

their tractors were modernized in ways besides just looks. Both Deere and Harvester had full lines of styled tractors from single-plow models to four-plow. And they had modern tillage, planting, and harvesting equipment to go with them.

The biggest competitive impact of the time, however, came in June of 1939. Henry Ford was back in the tractor business. The feature that made Ford's new Model 9N tractor so special was the draft-load compensating hydraulic three-point hitch. Ford had made an agreement with Harry Ferguson for the incorporation of Ferguson's system of mounted implements and patented hydraulics into his new tractor. With the Ferguson system (the hitch, hydraulics, and custom implements), the 2,500lb, $600 Ford-Ferguson could out perform tractors weighing and costing twice as much.

The Ford-Ferguson Model 9N was not a row-crop tractor, nor was it a standard tread. It had adjustable front and rear wheel spreads, and while it had fairly good crop clearance, it was low enough to be used for orchard duties. The 9N established the trend away from the row-crop configuration and toward what became known as the "utility" configuration.

Most in the tractor industry thought the 9N was just another Fordson and didn't take it too seriously. When sales for its first full year of production topped 35,000, however, they knew they had to react. The onset of World War II kept production figures for all artificially low and also prevented the development of new models. This

The Model GM was a wartime version of the Model G three-plow tractor. The G came out in 1937 and received Dreyfuss styling in 1942 along with the change in designation to GM (for modernized). This was a means of getting a price increase past the wartime price controls. This nicely restored GM appeared at the 1994 Freeport, Illinois, show.

A well restored 1944 "wartime" Model A at the Freeport, Illinois, show. The A was produced between 1934 and 1952. In addition to the row crop version shown, it was available in a standard tread version, an orchard version and an industrial version. Around 300,000 of all types were built.

gave Deere, and the other competitors, time to think about their counter attack.

World War II

Even before the United States was drawn into the war on December 7, 1941, the Office of Production Management was dictating the amount of civilian production farm equipment suppliers could produce. The formula used by that office favored the smaller implement makers over Harvester and Deere in most areas. This allowed Oliver and Minneapolis-Moline to close the gap on market share.

Already in 1940, Deere was making war materials for the Canadian war effort. In 1941, a separate company was formed, called the Iowa Transmission Company, as a Deere subsidiary. This company manufactured tank transmissions and final drives in the Waterloo plant. Later, Deere was a subcontractor to Cletrac, making

World War II saw Deere heavily involved in war production. This picture shows a Deere employee building tail wheel assemblies for the Republic P-47 fighter aircraft.

They also manufactured ammunition, tank transmissions, and built mobile laundry units to support the war effort.

the MG-1 military crawler tractor. They also manufactured ammunition, assembled tail wheel units for the Republic P-47 fighter, and built mobile laundry units to support the war effort.

Just as had happened in World War I, the government soon called on Deere & Company to supply managerial talent for the war effort. Deere President Charles Wiman was asked to come to Washington, assume the rank of Colonel, and to work on tank procurement for the Army's Ordinance Corp. He resigned the

Deere presidency in the spring of 1942. Burton Peek was elected president pro tem by the Deere board. The Peeks were related to John Deere through his wife, Demarius Lamb, so the family management tradition was carried during this period.

In the war years, many changes occurred in Deere & Company. Board member and former vice president Charles Webber, grandson of the founder, died, cutting one of the last ties of direct heritage. Webber had given sixty-seven years

Famous Industrial Designer Henry Dreyfuss is shown here at his desk in the Deere headquarters building. Dreyfuss' New York design firm was hired by Deere & Company in 1937 to style their line of tractors. The success of his initial efforts led to Dreyfuss' influence throughout the entire product line. Although Dreyfuss died in the early seventies, the relationship with his firm has lasted to the present time.

of service. Frank Silloway, Charles Stone, and Lawrence Murphy worked closely with Burton Peek as vice presidents. Originally, Stone and Murphy were responsible for manufacturing, and Silloway was in charge of sales. In 1944, Charles Stone assumed responsibility for product development, while Murphy handled manufacturing, engineering, and the laboratories. With these changes, Burton Peek reinstituted the policy of decentralization of control of the various out lying factories. Centralization had been adopted to expedite wartime production.

By the end of World War II, it was becoming fairly obvious to Deere management, and to other tractor manufacturers that the Ford-Ferguson was winning the battle for the hearts and minds of the farmers. The Ford-Ferguson, with its hydraulic three-point hitch for mounted implements, was selling for around the same price as the John Deere H. The squat little Ford, however, could plow twelve acres while an H did six.

For the years 1939 through 1947, Deere averaged about 25,000 tractors per year for the small-farm market. This number included Models B, L, LA, and H. In the same time, Ford-Ferguson sold an average 42,000 per year of their only model.

To counter Ford's inroad into the small farm marketplace, the John Deere Model M was born, replacing the L, LA, and the H. It was billed as a general-purpose utility tractor. The M came equipped with a gasoline-only, vertical, two-cylinder engine; a departure from the customary horizontal engine. It also had the three-point Touch-O-Matic rear implement hydraulic lift. The Touch-O-Matic lift was similar to the Ford-Ferguson system, except it did not incorporate Ferguson's automatic load compensating "draft control," thereby avoiding patent conflicts.

The Ms configuration did not satisfy all of Deere's customers, however, so in traditional Deere fashion the MT was added to the line in

The Model L was treated to Dreyfuss styling in 1938. An industrial version, the LI, was brought out in 1940. Its 10hp (belt) engine provided enough power for a single-bottom 12in plow.

1949. The MT was essentially the same tractor, but could be equipped with an adjustable wide-front, dual tricycle front, or single front wheel. Dual Touch-O-Matic was an added option, allowing independent control of right and left side implements.

Diesel Power

A heavily loaded Model D, or Model G, both with engines well over 400ci, could go through a lot of fuel in a day. Even at fifteen cents per gallon, the daily use of the better part of a barrel of kerosene could not be overlooked.

By the late 1930s, the use of fuel-efficient diesel engines was becoming routine. In tractors, Caterpillar, International Harvester, and Cletrac all offered diesels. In 1935, Deere Chief Engineer Barrett Rich concluded that diesel power was the wave of the future. Work began that year on various types of diesel engines.

A styled Model L pulls a one-row potato planter. The Model L was considered a replacement for three horses, and the more powerful Model LA was the equivalent of four horses.

The LA, as shown, can be distinguished from the L by the noticeably larger rear wheels. Although these tractors looked small, about the same as today's garden tractors, they were capable of serious farm work. During the early forties there were still many horses employed in routine farming, and each of these tractors was considered able to replace two teams.

By 1940, the diesel engine had progressed to where it was ready to go in a tractor. Eight experimental Model MX tractors were built. Testing continued to the end of 1941. The tractor was then completely redesigned to eliminate weaknesses. The new MX was ready in 1944. Testing again lasted into 1947, followed by another redesign, which then became Deere's first production diesel tractor, the Model R.

When the Model R was introduced in 1949, Deere marketing people were afraid customers would not accept the new diesel as a replacement for the aging Model D. Therefore the D was co-produced for four more years. Advertising of the day pointed out similarities between the two: the two-cylinder engine, the ruggedness, and the simplicity. Also advertised were the Model R's advantages over the D: diesel economy, all-gear drive (rather than chain drive as in the D), and a five-speed gearbox rather than three. It also had 21 percent more power, it weighed half again as much, and it could handle five plow bottoms rather than three or four. It had live PTO, hydraulics, and a comfortable bench seat. The Model R could plow a forty in a

A 1939 Model L tractor pulls a new John Deere wagon. The scene is the King Farm in Moline, Illinois. The diminutive Model L was a 10hp tractor designed to replace a team of horses. It sold for about $450.

twelve hour day on less than twenty-five gallons of diesel fuel. By contrast, a Model D would take two days and take three times as much fuel.

Management Succession

After a bout of ill health terminated his military career, Charles Wiman returned to the presidency of Deere in the fall of 1944. Wiman swung full force into his policy of management decentralization, which had been reversed during the war to accommodate the war effort production.

Life in the head office was never dull. When the war ended, much effort was spent in harness-

The Model BO Lindeman Crawler was a conversion of the BO wheel tractor to crawler tracks by the Lindeman Brothers of Yakima, Washington. Lindeman also made many specialized implements for the western orchard trade, such as this ripper. BO Lindeman Crawlers were available from 1939 to 1947.

A styled Model D tractor pulls a Model 36 combine in this November 1945 photo. The Model D was a 42 belt horsepower tractor. Deere acquired the Model 36 combine in the Caterpillar combine deal in 1936. It stayed in the Deere line-up until 1953.

A John Deere Model B powers a No. 7 sheller in this 1944 photo. The truck looks like a 1931 Chevrolet.

ing resources in converting back to farm implements. Demand for tractors and implements had been pent up during the war, so the supplier who could best meet requirements would be best positioned to get repeat business later on.

Deere management decided, rather than expand the Waterloo tractor facilities, a second facility would be added in Dubuque, Iowa. The new Model M tractor, replacement for the H, L, and LA would be made there. Also to be made in Dubuque were the new versions of the crawler. After the acquisition of Lindeman, crawlers based on the new M were to be assembled there.

Right after World War II, Charles Wiman, president of Deere & Company, made a fact-finding trip to the countries of Argentina and Peru. Wiman was impressed with the potential for implement and tractor business in those countries. That started Deere on a process of international expansion that would eventually see the company go worldwide.

In 1954, Charles Deere Wiman learned he had a terminal illness and only had months to live. As head of the company since the days of the GP tractor in 1928, Wiman's last major responsibility was to oversee the selection of his replacement. The company's predisposition to Deere family members was upwards in his mind, but such lineal decent was not considered sacrosanct by the Board. Nevertheless, of those related to John Deere by birth or by marriage, and of those within and without the company unrelated, William Hewitt, Wiman's son-in-law, was selected. On May 12, 1955, Wiman died.

The John Deere factory in Dubuque, Iowa, is shown in 1947 after the beginning of tractor production there. It originally had 600,000 square feet of floor space. The compact Model M utility tractor was the first to be built in Dubuque.

After World War II, Deere & Company began using aircraft in a big way to visit customers and their far-flung factories. This scene from the Moline airport in 1947 shows Deere's line-up of what are now considered the ultimate in classic planes. From left to right, behind the LA-I tractor are a Fairchild PT-26 Cornell, a North American Navion, a Grumman G-44 Widgeon amphibian and a Beechcraft Model 18.

Deere & Company purchased the Killefer Manufacturing Corporation of Los Angeles in 1937. Killefer was noted for deep tillage equipment, such as subsoilers, disks, and pan breakers. This 1947 photo shows a Model G tractor pulling a No. 970 Killefer disk tiller.

Fortune Magazine ran an article on the leadership transition at Deere. Mr. Hewitt's attributes for the position, the article pointed out, were more real than hereditary. At the age of forty he was young but had experience in the business. He had begun his career with Ford-Ferguson, and after his marriage to Wiman's daughter, served in a Deere branch office. He was a graduate of the University of California at Berkeley—college graduates were not that common in Deere management at that time, Wiman himself being an exception. And he had had a distinguished Navy tour during World War II, rising to the rank of Lieutenant Commander. The *Fortune* article went on to say that Hewitt's associates within Deere & Company regarded him

By late 1947, the second generation of Dreyfuss styled tractors, had emerged. Shown here is the big Model G. About the only difference between early and late styled Gs was in the bench seat used on the late models. It is shown here with a four-row cultivator.

A Model M and a late-styled Model A pull Lindeman Landshapers near Lindeman's Yakima, Washington, plant in July of 1948. Deere had purchased Lindeman Power Equipment Company in 1946.

A late-styled Model B, with the pressed steel frame and round-top fenders operates a PTO binder in the Canadian wheat fields in 1948. Well into the 1950s, in many areas, farmers preferred binding, shocking, and threshing to the use of the new combines.

A late-styled John Deere Model B drives the fan load at the Stephenson County Antique Engine Show in Freeport, Illinois. The fan, or air brake, loads the engine so adjustments can be made for maximum power. Collectors bring their tractors to shows such as this to show off their work to the public. *Robert N. Pripps*

highly for his friendly personality, leadership, and coolness under pressure. William A. Hewitt assumed the presidency of Deere in 1955.

The New Generation

Early in 1953, Deere management people turned their thoughts to tractor engines with more than two cylinders. The handwriting, they realized, was on the wall: despite their market niche, and all the touted advantages of the two-cylinder engine, its limits had been reached. The question was not whether, but when, for the larger tractors. Another question was whether to switch only the diesels, or to change the entire line at one time.

The two-cylinder engine was known for its simplicity, long life, and fuel economy; factors that are always requirements of a tractor engine. Nevertheless, as the 1960s approached, the two-cylinder engine was restricting tractor design. Limits were reached as far as increasing horse-

power was concerned, and it was predicted that horsepower requirements would double and even triple in the next decade.

A late-styled Model A "Puller" after its turn at the weight sled at the Freeport, Illinois, show in 1994. Late-styled As had the pressed steel frame.

161

With the introduction of the Model 435 diesel tractor in 1959, the last of the two-cylinders was born (which, interestingly, was a two-cycle engine made by GM). It was the end of a long, proud line.

With all the secrecy of the Manhattan Project, select engineers were pulled from their assignments and sent to a remote site. What followed was one of the best-kept non-governmental corporate undercover operations in history. The Deere "Butcher Shop Boys" (they were set up in a former grocery store building) were assigned the task of designing a "New Generation" of tractors. These tractors were to have all-new

The 1949 John Deere Model MC was the first all-John Deere crawler. The conversion was done by Lindeman, which had been a division of John Deere since 1946. The lightweight MC was especially useful for light construction and landscaping.

multi-cylinder engines. They were to be ready for introduction in 1960. For export, however, the Model 730 two-cylinder diesel was built in Waterloo until early 1961. The 730 was also built in Argentina throughout the 1960s.

August 30, 1960, with hoopla rivaled only by the Super Bowl, the "New Generation" John Deere tractors were unveiled at the Coliseum in Dallas, Texas, at an event known as Deere Day in Dallas. Deere flew in dealers and press people from all across the country. There were fireworks and barbecues and big-name entertainers.

The new line of Dreyfuss styled multi-cylinder tractors was an unqualified success. The dealers liked them, and the farmers bought them. Sales for 1961 and 1962 were up dramatically.

There were four models in the new line: the 1010 at 30 drawbar horsepower, the 2010 at 40

The Model R was John Deere's first diesel. It was a two-cylinder type, just like the previous spark-ignition kerosene burners. The Model R was capable of 46 drawbar horsepower and was built from 1949 to 1954.

The Model R was John Deere's first diesel tractor. It used a gasoline pony motor for starting. It was designed to be a replacement for the venerable Model D, but the D's pop- ularity kept it in production until 1953. The R was built between 1949 and 1954. Shown is a 1952 model owned by Jon Davis of Maplewood, Ohio. *Andrew Morland*

drawbar horsepower, the 3010 at 55 drawbar horsepower, and the 4010 at 80 drawbar horsepower. Most were available with gasoline, diesel, or LPG (liquefied petroleum gas) engines. They were available in a variety of configurations from utility to row-crop. The 1010 was even available as a crawler.

Industrial Equipment Division

The Industrial Equipment Division was established in 1956. A separate dealer and marketing organization was established. Finally, a separate engineering department was added.

By 1962, a complete new line of equipment was introduced; the JD line. All model designations began with the letters "JD." Equipment included motor graders, logging devices, loaders, backhoes, and crawlers.

Consumer Products Division

The old Van Brunt operation in Horicon, Wisconsin, was now called the Horicon Works. In 1963, a homeowner-type lawn tractor, called the Model 110, was built there. It used a seven horsepower single cylinder Kohler engine. From that humble beginning, Deere has become the world's largest producer of such items. In addition, an astounding variety of consumer products has also been forthcoming from the Horicon plant. The list includes chain saws, snowmobiles, mowers, bicycles, snow blowers, and all-terrain work vehicles.

By 1949, the venerable Model D had carried the load for the large-acreage wheat farmers for almost thirty years. Now more power was needed than even the upgraded D could provide. At the same time, the fuel consumption of the large-displacement, low-compression kerosene burners was becoming a problem. Deere's answer to both concerns was the all-new Model R. A restored example is shown here at the John Deere Historic Site in Grand Detour in 1993.

This 1949 photo shows a Model R tractor pulling a No. 36 combine, which had its own six-cylinder engine. It was available in level land, hillside, and extreme-hillside versions.

The Model MT, a variation of the M, was brought out in 1949. It featured a convertible front end arrangement that could accommodate a tricycle, single, or wide-front front wheel setup. Shown is a 1950 Model MT owned by Dale Crawford of Davis, Illinois.

The Model 40 was one of the niftiest small tractors of the period. It was built from 1953 to 1956. It was rated at 22 PTO hp. Built in the Dubuque factory, the Model 40 was originally available as the standard, the tricycle (as shown), and the 40C crawler. Other variations were soon added in the true John Deere tradition of giving the customer what he (or she) wanted. These included the high-crop, utility, two-row utility, and a low-clearance "special."

Deere & Company had a combine that was readied for market in the late 1920s. Coincidentally, Caterpillar had just been formed by the merger of Best and Holt. Caterpillar offered to sell its Western Harvester Division's line of fairly successful combines, located in Stockton, California, to Deere. The price was too steep for Deere, who decided to pass up the offer. In 1935, Caterpillar purposed a joint dealership arrangement, and offered to throw in the rights to their hillside combine. Deere's several varieties were level-land models. The Model 33 combine shown in this 1952 photo was added to the line in 1940. It is being pulled by a Caterpillar D-4 tractor.

A series of John Deere Model 36B combines are shown in a vast wheat field in Eastern Washington being pulled by Caterpillar D-6s and D-7s. The Model 36 was originally built by Holt. It stayed in the Deere line into the fifties.

Before World War II, Deere & Company began working on PTO-driven combines. The first of these was the No. 6. Next came the 10, 11, and 12, with 3.5, 5, and 6ft cuts, respectively. The "A" versions of each were added in 1940 with left hand cutters. The No. 12A, shown in this 1951 photo, proved to be very popular and stayed in the line until 1952. The tractor is a late-styled Model B.

A late-styled Model B pulls a No. 594 side-delivery rake in this 1951 photo. The late-styled Model B used a 175ci two-cylinder engine which produced 28hp on the belt.

A Model 65 Combine is pulled through Canadian wheat by a Model AR tractor in 1951. The 65 was a pulled version of the Model 55 self-propelled combine. The AR was a standard tread version of the Model A tractor.

The Model 50 replaced the Model B tractor in late 1952. The "Numbered Series" tractors, which included the Model 50, featured live hydraulics and a live PTO. The Model 50 was slightly more powerful than the Model B and was capable of 31hp on the belt.

The early Numbered Series tractors, such as this restored Model 50, retained the simple green painted sheet metal with yellow wheels combination. Many collectors feel these were the most handsome of all the John Deeres. This Model 50 was seen at the 1994 Franklin Grove, Illinois, show.

The Model 60 replaced the Model A tractor in 1952 and stayed in the line until 1956. It is shown here with a three-point hitch using the new Powr-Trol hydraulic system.

The Model 70 was a replacement for the mighty Model G. A flex planter with a No. 850 bedder is being carried. Originally offered with all-fuel, gasoline, or LPG engines, a diesel option was included in 1954.

Next page
This John Deere ad from 1953 touts the Model 70 as the latest "rung of achievement."

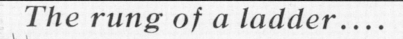

The rung of a ladder....

*"The rung of a ladder was never meant
to rest upon, but only to hold a man's foot
long enough to enable him to put the other
somewhat higher."*

—*Thomas Huxley*

Those eloquent lines embody a principle that has been followed at John Deere for more than a century.

Pausing on each rung just long enough to make sure of their footing, John Deere engineers, for instance, are climbing ever upward, finding new ways to speed up your farming . . . to lighten your work . . . to increase your profits.

The results, of course, are manifold. But none are more valued than farmer respect and enthusiasm for John Deere products, which—in 116 years of service to American agriculture—have never been higher than they are today. And by this very measure, recent progress in the design and manufacture of John Deere Farm Equipment has been particularly outstanding.

The latest "rung of achievement" is the Model "70" Tractor, shown below. An important new member of a famous family, the John Deere Model "70" is a powerful tractor, with feature after feature that proclaim it the modern tractor for the large row-crop farm . . . a tractor that continues and accentuates the famed John Deere policy of offering farmers across the nation the utmost in modern design and proved performance . . . in quality farm equipment.

*Drop in and see your John Deere dealer. He'll be glad to show you
the Model "70" and tell you all about the many other new and field-
proved machines in today's John Deere line of quality farm equipment.*

Shown here is a Model 70 high-crop diesel row-crop. The Model 70 was also available in a standard tread version. This photo was taken in 1955.

A DT-3 disk tiller, pulled by a D7 Caterpillar, operates near Blythe, California. Disk tillers were made in the Killefer works in California.

William Hewitt took over as president of Deere & Company in 1955. It was Hewitt who presided over the successful transition to "The New Generation" tractors; tractors with engines with more than two cylinders. Hewitt was the son-in-law of Charles Deere Wiman, and the last of the Deere family members to head the company. Hewitt's attributes for the position were more than just hereditary; he was well educated, experienced, and had a contagious good humor that endeared him to those around him

A John Deere Model 70 Standard Diesel. Its engine produced a maximum 51 PTO horsepower. The Model 70 Standard was unique among standard tread John Deere tractors up to that time in that it was the same as the row crop except for the axles and fenders.

John Deere Van Brunt twenty-four-row grain drills are shown in this 1957 picture. The Van Brunt works in Horicon, Wisconsin, was acquired by Deere in 1911 in order to gain seeder and drill capability. The tractor is an 820 diesel.

THE JOHN DEERE 45 EDIBLE BEAN COMBINE

GIVES YOU MORE AND CLEANER BEANS WITHOUT CRACKING

The John Deere Model 45 combine was Deere's second self-propelled combine. It was introduced in 1957. It initially was powered by a Hercules engine, but later, a Deere engine of 42hp was fitted. Shown is the edible bean configuration.

A Model 50 tractor with a mounted No. 101 single row corn picker is shown in this November 1951 photo. The Model 50 tractor replaced the Model B during the 1952 model year. It was rated at 26 PTO horsepower.

The Twenty Series tractors came out in 1956. They stayed in production until 1958. They generally replaced the Numbered Series. The big improvement feature was the load-compensating three-point hitch, called Custom Powr-Trol. The smallest of the Twenty Series was the Model 320, shown here. It was aimed at truck gardeners and small farmers. This restored 320 is shown at the Grand Detour historic site.

The Model 320 had the power to handle a No. 415 two-bottom plow, as shown in this 1956 photo. The 100.5ci engine produced a maximum of 24.9hp at the PTO.

The Model 420 was introduced in 1956 to replace the Model 40. It had many improvements including a 20 percent power increase. It was available in eight configura-tions such as the 420H high-crop shown here with an al-falfa sprayer. Note the several small engines on top of the spray rig.

The Model 420C crawler was a more mature tractor than the 40C it replaced. It is shown here with a No. 62 dozer.

The 420C was beefed up to handle heavier chores being assigned it in construction and forestry. It was available with either a four-roller or five-roller undercarriage. This one, with a five-roller undercarriage is equipped with a No. 90 loader and a ripper on the three-point hitch.

The Model 520 continued the tradition of the Model B tractor. This one is shown with a disc harrow on its three-point hitch.

The Model 620 replaced the Model 60 tractor in 1956. The 620, shown here with a KBA disk, was rated at 34 drawbar horsepower during Nebraska tests.

A Model 620 tractor is shown here in this 1957 photo with a Model 30 PTO combine. The Model 30 was introduced in 1956. It had a 7ft cutter.

The Model 720 was available in gasoline, all-fuel, LPG, and diesel versions. It was also available in row-crop, high-crop, and standard tread configurations. Shown here is a 720 row-crop diesel with a 14T baler and bale chucker. Amateur farmer friends of the author began baling with such a rig. One, who weighed about 140lbs, rode on the trailer and had the idea that he was supposed to catch the bales.

The Model 820 tractor was a replacement for the Model R and Model 80 standard tread tractors. It was available in diesel power only. It is shown here with the last of the PTO combines, the Model 65.

The Thirty Series came out in 1958 and was available through 1960. The line included replacements for each of the Twenty Series tractors. Shown here is the 430S Standard with 4110 cultivator.

The 430 also came in a LPG model. This one is shown pulling a 5ft disk. One of the features of the 430 was a direction reverser for forward and backward travel in each gear.

Lyle Pals single front wheel John Deere 530 is a 1958 model. It is equipped with power steering and Custom Powr-Trol load compensating three-point hitch. Pals has a collection of more than thirty rare and common John Deere two-cylinder tractors. Pals also farms some 2,000 acres near Egan, Illinois. *Andrew Morland*

The Thirty Series tractors had a revised color scheme with more yellow on the sheet metal. The 530 shown here has power-adjusted rear wheel width. It is pulling a No. 896 side-delivery rake.

A Model 530 tractor operates with a No. 30 potato digger near Bay City, Michigan, in 1958.

A Model 530 tractor operates a No. 8 PTO mower.

The Model 630 was the ultimate extension of the Model A line. It was built from 1958 through 1960 and could be equipped to burn distillate fuel, gasoline, or liquefied petroleum gas. It was in the 50hp class. This restored example appeared at the Waukee, Iowa, show in 1994.

Picking stones was not done like this when the author was a boy! In this 1959 photo, a Model 630 tractor oper- ates a No. 30 potato picker with a stone picker attachment.

The Model 630 was available in gasoline, all-fuel, and LPG versions. The LPG type is shown here with a No. 484 planter.

The last of the two-cylinder tractors, the Model 435 was introduced in 1959 and only built through 1960. Rather than the traditional Deere engine, the 435 used a GM two-cycle diesel with a supercharger. It was rated at 28 PTO horsepower. Shown in the cockpit is owner Don Wolf. *Andrew Morland*

In the 1950s Deere picked up the patent rights to the Lundell-type forage harvester. Flails cut the crop which was then fed into a blower with blades to further chop the stalks. Shown behind the Model 630 tractor is a No. 12 forage harvester. It is feeding the material into a No. 110 Chuck Wagon.

By 1969, when this photo was taken, diesel engines were greatly preferred for the larger tractors. Shown here is a 730 diesel with a No. 810 plow.

The Model 730 was so popular that some were built in Waterloo during 1961 after the introduction of the New Generation tractors. Also, the Model 730 was built throughout the 1960s in Argentina. A 730 is shown here with a No. 66 five-bottom plow.

The 730 Standard was not much different from the row-crop version; just different wheels, axles, and fenders.

The big Model 830 tractor was the ultimate two-cylinder. At over four tons, it was also the biggest. The 830 offered the option of a V-4 pony motor or electric starter.

Called Mister Mighty in Deere advertising, the 830 was a big and powerful tractor. It was available only in the standard tread configuration and only as a diesel.

The last new two-cylinder, the John Deere Model 435 tractor came out in 1959 and was sold through 1960. The 435 was a diesel, but not like other Deere diesels. The 435 used a General Motors 2-53 two-cylinder two cycle engine with a blower. Otherwise, the tractor was much like the 430. Nebraska tests of the 435 yielded ratings of 29.41 at the drawbar and 32.91 on the PTO. The 435 was the first John Deere tractor to be offered with either a 540, or 1000rpm PTO.

When the Industrial Equipment Division of Deere & Company was established in 1956, the company went after the construction equipment business in a big way. Shown here is an 1958 version of what would become the Model 840 (it appears the number has been added to the photo after the fact). The Model 840 was a derivation of the 830 which was sold as a unit with either a Hancock self-loading scraper or with a Deere 400 elevating scraper. The 840s were sold through 1964 and were the last of the two-cylinders built for the domestic market.

Cotton pickers were added to the Deere line in 1958. Shown here is a 1960 version of the large self-propelled version, the Model 99. It could pick the same amount as of eighty hand pickers.

Deere President William Hewitt (left) and Architect Eero Saarinen look over a model of the new headquarters building in 1960. The first of these offices were occupied in 1964.

The giant John Deere 8010 was shown to farmers at a Deere field day near Marshalltown, Iowa, in the fall of 1959. It was the first John Deere tractor with more than two cylinders (it had six) since the Dain-John Deere of 1916. The number of cylinders and the designation, 8010, might have tipped off the farmers that more changes were coming. There is no indication they were suspicious, however.

The articulated, six-cylinder John Deere Model 8010 was big in anyone's book. Its working weight was about 25,000lbs; it was over 8ft tall; it had air brakes, and a 24V electrical system. The diesel engine produced 215hp. In 1960, an improved version, the 8020, was introduced.

Deere Day in Dallas, August 29, 1960. More than 100 airplanes from seventy-five cities brought 6,000 John Deere dealers to Dallas for the unveiling of the "New Generation." Deere & Company had assembled 136 new multi-cylinder tractors and 324 pieces of other equipment for the amazement of the dealers. The scene is the Cotton Bowl stadium.

The Dreyfuss-styled "New Generation" tractors announced in Dallas in the fall of 1960 consisted of two lines from Dubuque and two from Waterloo. The 35hp Model 1010 and the 45hp Model 2010 were from Dubuque and had four-cylinder engines. From Waterloo came the six-cylinder, 80hp 4010 and the four-cylinder, 55hp, Model 3010, as shown in this photo with a Model 30 combine.

Claimed to be the most copied tractor in the world, the 80hp six-cylinder Model 4010 had 37 percent more power than the old two-cylinder Model 730, but only weighed 3 percent more. It is shown here with a beet harvester.

A Model 1010C crawler with a winch dray and a clutch of logs is shown in this 1962 photo. The 1010C was based on the Dubuque-built 1010 wheel tractor. Its four-cylinder 144.5ci engine produced a maximum of 36hp PTO horsepower. The 1010C weighed about 7,500lbs without the winch or dozer blade. During Nebraska testing, the 1010C recorded a drawbar pull of 7484lbs.

Styled by Henry Dreyfuss and numbered with the other New Generation tractors, the Model 110 Lawn and Garden tractor was a product of the John Deere Horicon Works. Design work began in the late 1950s, but Deere headquarters people were not inclined to add it to the line because of all the effort being expended on the farm tractors. Horicon sales and engineering people persisted, however, and production of the Model 110 began in late 1962, although it was actually well into 1963 before they were available for sale. The Model 110 was powered by a one-cylinder air-cooled Kohler engine of 7hp.

Chapter 6

Industry Leadership:
1962-Present

"Deere men have a more romantic orientation. They honestly
feel that Deere deserves their fealty and reverence. This view is not
exactly fashionable. But it has stood the test of time."
Management Today, 1973

International Scope

When William Hewitt took over as president of Deere & Company in 1955, he brought with him a sense of urgency for international expansion. This sense was shared by some of the other younger board members. By 1956, a branch was established in Mexico and a new company formed, John Deere CA, to handle South and Central American expansion. In 1958, tractors were being built in Monterey, Mexico.

Even prior to Hewitt's rise to the presidency, the board had received a proposal from some German bankers to buy controlling interest in the German company, Heinrich Lanz, of Mannheim. In 1953, the board of Deere & Company decided against picking up Lanz, one of the two prominent German implement makers, for financial reasons. In 1956, however, Deere took another look at Lanz and decided to go ahead.

The Lanz line consisted of nineteen tractor models, from 11hp to 60hp. Also produced were PTO and self-propelled combines and other implements. The number of tractors, nicknamed "Bulldogs," was reduced to thirteen by 1957, and they were by then painted John Deere green and yellow. During 1960, new models were introduced along the lines of the U.S. New Generation tractors.

Lanz had factory connections in Spain, which now belonged to Deere. At this time, Deere also began operations in France.

The Worldwide Tractor

In the early sixties, several of the leading farm equipment companies, had adopted standardized products to be built in all of their far-flung operations. In 1963, Deere & Company followed suit. The company now had manufacturing facilities in Spain, Germany, France, Argentina, Mexico, and South Africa, as well as those in the U.S. and Canada.

By 1965, three new versions of the standard, or Worldwide, tractor were introduced: the Model 310, a three-cylinder diesel of 32hp; the Model 510, also a three-cylinder diesel, but with 40hp; and the Model 710 at 50hp, using a four-cylinder diesel engine.

The Administrative Center

Just as Dreyfuss styling brought technical credit to Deere tractors in 1938, so William Hewitt recognized that architectural excellence in the headquarters facility would ultimately be reflected in product quality and company profitability. Deere facilities had always reflected Midwest practicality and plain functionalism. Hewitt reasoned that employees saw themselves

The Rusty Palace. This is the name given to the Deere & Company headquarters building because of the use of an external corrosion-limiting steel structure and the luxurious feeling given to the interior space as a result of the view provided by the glass walls and the extensive landscaping. Famous architect Eero Saarinen designed the structure at the request of Chairman Hewitt. Hewitt instructed Saarinen to keep in mind not only the rugged, honest, close-to-the-soil men who created the company and helped it to grow, but the farmers, dealers, suppliers, and present and future employees, who are also down to earth people. The $8 million structure was first occupied in 1964. There are three parts to the building: a main office building, an auditorium-product display building, and the West Office Building. The entire complex, which sits on a 1,000 acre plot about seventy miles downstream from the Grand Detour blacksmith shop, is known as the Deere & Company World Headquarters and Administrative Center.

in the same way, and not in the worldwide industry leader role. Accordingly, when new headquarters facilities were authorized by the board in 1957, Hewitt sought outstanding architectural talent to do the design work. World renown architect Eero Saarinen was retained and given the challenge of designing a thoroughly modern complex without being especially sophisticated or glossy. Instead it was to be down to earth and rugged, befitting men of the soil.

Robert A. Hanson was named Executive Vice President in 1975 and took over as chairman, president, and chief executive officer of Deere & Company from William Hewitt in 1982. Hewitt was the last member of the Deere family to head the company. Hanson had come up through the ranks of the company, and had experience in the international phases of the operation. Hanson was a strong and enthusiastic leader who took the company through some times of devastating depression in the construction and farm machinery businesses. Hanson retired in 1990 and was replaced by the current chairman, Hans Becherer, another long-time Deere man who worked his way up through the Overseas Division.

Since it opened in 1964, the Administrative Center, designed by the late Eero Saarinen, has won a number of awards for excellence and innovation.

The Administrative Center consists of a main office building, a 400-seat auditorium, a product display building, and the West Office Building. It provides space for about 2,000 employees. The main office building sits across a wooded ravine with the product display and auditorium buildings to the east. The West Office Building is on a plateau to the west. Both are

Tractors being assembled in the Mannheim, Germany, factory. Deere & Company acquired Heinrich Lanz A.G., of Mannheim in 1956. Lanz had been a pioneer in the European tractor business since 1911 and was noted for the Bulldog tractor, introduced in 1921, and the general purpose Allwork tractor of 1939. A new tractor, the Alldog, was brought out in 1951. At the time of this photo, 1963, two new Deere-Lanz tractors were being assembled: the 300 and the 500.

connected to the main office building by glass bridges. Surrounding the buildings are lakes and landscaping and sculptures. Inside there is a collection of art, sculpture and antiques, both in the office areas and on the display floor.

Architect Saarinen said of the facility he designed, "We tried to get into these buildings the character of John Deere products, the Company, the customers it serves, and the friendly informal attitude of its personnel." It's fair to say he accomplished his goal and captured the essence of the mystique that is John Deere.

World Leadership

In 1963, Deere & Company passed International Harvester as the number one producer of agricultural equipment. In the fall of that year, the 3020 and 4020 models were announced; upgrades of the 3010 and 4010 New Generation tractors of 1960. The 4020 has become a classic in its own right, being the most produced John Deere tractor since the two-cylinder models (which had production runs of as many as thirty years). The Models 1020, 2020, and 5020 were added later to round out the line.

The year 1964 was "the best yet," for Deere & Company. It was also a peak in profitability for some time to come. Foreign operations became a drain, rather than a help for the corporation for the next eight years. In Germany, the problem was especially acute, as the Lanz operation had been struggling to be competitive be-

The first Lanz Bulldog tractor of 1911. It featured a single-cylinder engine with a dissipative (hopper) cooling system. This tractor had hard rubber tires and "external" brakes. Deere & Company acquired Heinrich Lanz A.G., of Mannheim, in 1956.

Lanz tractors built at Mannheim were painted green and yellow from 1957 and on. For 1960, two new Deere-Lanz Dreyfuss and Associates styled tractors were announced: the 300 and the 500 shown here. These were 28hp and 36hp tractors respectively, which used a Lanz ten-speed transmission and a four-cylinder engine from the 1010 Dubuque tractor.

A 4010 LP tractor works with an 870 six-row integral lister and planter. The 4010 was a six-cylinder tractor of 80hp

fore the acquisition. The company entertained the possibility of mergers and joint ventures during these lean years with first Deutz of Germany, and later Fiat of Italy. In the end, however, it was decided to remain independent. More tractor production was shifted from the U.S. to Mannheim, to take up the slack there.

The Australian Connection

In 1970, Deere & Company expanded their sphere of influence into the land down under. A new company was established: Chamberlain John Deere Pty. Ltd. Deere & Company owned 49 percent. Chamberlain had been in the tractor and implement business in Australia since 1948, making a line of two-cylinder tractors with horizontally opposed cylinders.

Chamberlain continued to make and sell its own brand of yellow tractors, plus import other tractor models and implements for assembly in-country, from Deere's worldwide operations.

Worldwide Industry Problems

The 1970s produced some world-shaking upheavals. First came massive grain buys by the Soviet Union, which tended to disrupt the normal balance of farm stability in supply and demand. This was followed by the oil embargo of 1973, and the resulting tripling of American fuel prices. At the end of the decade, a grain embargo was imposed by the United States on the Soviet union in retaliation for their invasion of Afghanistan, which again upset supply and demand. During the boom times of the seventies,

A 1962 industrial version of the big 4010 80hp tractor equipped with a farm loader. The 4010 was the most popular of the New Generation tractors.

farmers leveraged themselves into more land and larger equipment with borrowed money. Interest rates rose to an astronomical 18 percent.

With the 1980s, inflationary pressures were brought under control, but land values fell, as did farm prices. Many a hapless farmer found himself the victim of too much government intervention in his business and went bankrupt. This of course hurt the implement companies at the same time. International Harvester was forced into a merger with a foundering Case. Ford first tried to acquire prosperity by picking up New Holland and then Canadian Versatile, but in the end, sold out to Fiat. Massey-Ferguson survived with massive infusions of aid from the British and Canadian governments. White Farm Equipment, the repository of the Oliver, Minneapolis-Moline, and Cockshutt heritages, survived after acquisition by several different holding companies. Deere & Company went through some extremely difficult times, but had the management talent and financial strength to come through in an even stronger position.

Yanmar

By 1976, Deere & Company's smallest farm tractor was the 40hp Model 2040. Several other manufacturers had smaller tractors for the hobby farmer, but Deere was not represented in that market. Horicon tractors, for the home owner, were then in the 7-15hp class. These were belt-driven single cylinder units designed for mowing and snow blowing, not for serious farm work.

Recognizing a market in the U.S. alone of some 40,000 units per year, the Horicon people were commissioned to look into a tractor in the 20-30hp range, with a diesel engine and all-gear drive.

It was at this time that Kubota, of Japan, began to market a compact diesel tractor in the U.S market. Its success prompted other Japanese companies to also get involved. By 1977, Japan

The 30 Series tractors, known as Generation II, were introduced in the fall of 1971. The first of these to make the scene was the 2030, replacing the 2020. It was available in gasoline and diesel versions, both of which were rated at 60hp. The 2030 was the last new farm tractor available with a gasoline engine, and that option was dropped in 1973.

was selling more tractors in the under 30hp market in the U.S. than U.S. makers. The results of the Horicon study indicated the domestic tractor would be too expensive to compete.

Deere & Company already had a relationship with Yanmar, a major Japanese diesel engine maker, through which it had been marketing to Japan. Arrangements were made for a joint Deere-Yanmar company to manufacture tractors to John Deere specifications. Deere would also market some Yanmar tractors already being made under the John Deere name. Thus, Deere soon acquired a competitive line of tractors from 11-30 horsepower.

New Products for the Eighties

One of the most remarkable new devices to come out of Deere & Company during this period was the Max-Emerge planter. With ever widening rows of seed planting, a planter malfunction was the dread of every farmer. The failure would often not be recognized until the crop failed to come up. Deere engineers developed a new concept planter. It not only placed the seed in the ground with the right amount of soil depth and pressure, it also electronically checked each row's operation. If seeds failed to come out, the operator was warned immediately.

Deere combines garnered over 40 percent of the U.S. market by 1980 and Deere & Company adopted a conservative policy regarding changes. New Holland had introduced a new rotary-type combine, but it did not work as well as the shaker-type in some conditions. Therefore, Deere resisted changing, although many experiments were conducted. The 900 series combines for the European market employed a "cross-shaker" design which helped eliminate the heavy straw.

A new concept in manure spreaders was also developed. It was called the "hydrapush" spreader. It used hydraulic power to move the manure back to the spreader mechanism, rather than the

This No. 1600 chisel plow is making the 1971 Model 4620 tractor snort. The 4620 was a turbocharged, intercooled, 135hp machine. It is shown here with the optional Sound-Gard Body. Chisel plowing leaves the field surface rough for the retention of top soil and snow.

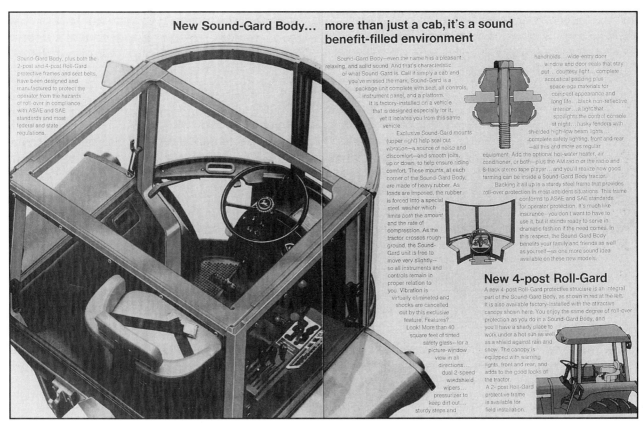

New Sound-Gard Body... more than just a cab, it's a sound benefit-filled environment

Sound-Gard Body, plus both the 2-post and 4-post Roll-Gard protective frames and seat belts, have been designed and manufactured to protect the operator from the hazards of roll-over in compliance with ASAE and SAE standards and most federal and state regulations.

Sound-Gard Body—even the name has a pleasant, relaxing, and solid sound. And that's characteristic of what Sound-Gard is. Call it simply a cab and you've missed the mark. Sound-Gard is a package unit complete with seat, all controls, instrument panel, and a platform. It is factory-installed on a vehicle that is designed especially for it, yet it isolates you from this same vehicle.

Exclusive Sound-Gard mounts (upper right) help seal out vibration—a source of noise and discomfort—and smooth jolts, up or down, to help ensure riding comfort. These mounts, at each corner of the Sound-Gard Body, are made of heavy rubber. As loads are imposed, the rubber is forced into a special steel washer which limits *both* the *amount* and the *rate* of compression. As the tractor crosses rough ground, the Sound-Gard unit is free to move very slightly—so all instruments and controls remain in proper relation to you. Vibration is virtually eliminated and shocks are cancelled out by this exclusive feature. Features? Look! More than 40 square feet of tinted safety glass—for a picture-window view in all directions... dual 2-speed windshield wipers... pressurizer to keep dirt out... sturdy steps and

handholds... wide-entry door window and door seals that stay put... courtesy light... complete acoustical padding plus space-age materials for compact appearance and long life... black non-reflective interior... a light that spotlights the control console at night... husky fenders with shielded high-low beam lights complete safety lighting, front and rear —all this and more as regular equipment. Add the optional hot-water heater, air conditioner, or both—plus the AM radio or the radio and 8-track stereo tape player... and you'll realize how good farming can be inside a Sound-Gard Body tractor.

Backing it all up is a sturdy steel frame that provides roll-over protection in most accident situations. This frame conforms to ASAE and SAE standards for operator protection. It's much like insurance—you don't want to have to use it, but it stands ready to serve in dramatic fashion if the need comes. In this respect, the Sound-Gard Body benefits your family and friends as well as yourself—as one more sound idea available on these new models.

New 4-post Roll-Gard

A new 4-post Roll-Gard protective structure is an integral part of the Sound-Gard Body, as shown in red at the left. It is also available factory-installed with the attractive canopy shown here. You enjoy the same degree of roll-over protection as you do in a Sound-Gard Body, and you'll have a shady place to work under a hot sun as well as a shield against rain and snow. The canopy is equipped with warning lights, front and rear, and adds to the good looks of the tractor. A 2-post Roll-Gard protective frame is available for field installation.

The Sound-Gard Body was announced in a two-page spread in the September-October Corn-Belt Edition of *The Furrow*. The new cab was a great advance in safety and comfort.

The John Deere 509 rotary mowers were introduced in 1972. The 509 was for heavy-duty mowing, and the 506, which was brought out in 1978, was for regular-duty mowing. The 503 was called an economy mower and came on the market in 1986. All provided a 5ft cut.

chain-link conveyor. Chain links often failed during cold weather; the "hydrapush" concept eliminated that problem.

Tractors for the Eighties and Nineties

Actually announced in 1977, but improved for the eighties, was the "Iron Horse" series with thirteen models. The subsequent 50-Series ran to sixteen models. It was followed by the 55-Series, the 60 Series and the current 6000-Series with a plethora of variations on the model theme. Mechanical front wheel drives (MFWD) were common and in 1982, castor action MFWD was introduced. This allowed much tighter cornering than previous front wheel drive systems.

The articulated four-wheel drive tractor had been pioneered by Steiger and Wagner in the mid-1950s. In 1959, John Deere introduced their first version, the 215hp Model 8010 (in 1960 called the 8020 after some improvements were made). Production ended in 1964. It wasn't until 1971 that another true John Deere articu-

lated tractor, the Model 7020, was offered. In the meantime, two models of articulated tractors, the WA-14 and WA-17, were made for John Deere by Wagner.

The 7020 was unlike any previous tractor of the articulated type in that wheel spacing was adjustable for row-crop work. The 7520 was essentially the same as the 7020, except a larger engine gave it more horsepower. Both were Waterloo tractors.

The 8430 and the 8630 were 1975 models. Articulated four-wheel drive tractors were maturing with the introduction of these two Waterloo-built monsters. As is the general case with new tractors, more power is offered than was provided by their predecessors. With these two, increased cylinder bore raised the displacement to effect the power increase.

Next came the 8440 and 8640 in 1979. Most of the improvements of these two new models over the ones they replaced were internal. These included new, stronger, quieter transmis-

Shown here is a 1972 150hp Model 4630 tractor with a No. 220 spray rig. It is also pulling a No. 1100 Culti-planter. It was available with hydrostatic front wheel drive.

sions and final-drive gears; increased lift capacity; front and rear differential locks; and on the 8640, new, stronger engine components. A computerized monitoring system, called the Investigator, warned of malfunctions. Several improvements provided a smoother ride for the operator; a welcome change because of the long hours of use these machines got per day.

Two 1980 diesel tractors from Yanmar were billed as the "Little Big Tractors," because of their small size and their big tractor features. They had three-cylinder engines; 22hp for the 850 and 27hp for the 950, of a mere 78ci and 105ci respectively. Featured were two-stick manual transmissions providing eight forward speeds, a differential lock, a category 1 hitch and optional mechanical front wheel drive.

The Model 1050 was added to the Yanmar-built line in 1980. It was essentially the same as the 950, except it was turbocharged. The 1050 had a rating of 33 PTO horsepower.

In 1981, the Yanmar-built Models 650 and 750 were added to the line-up. These compact tractors also had many of the big tractor features, but were generally considered estate or landscape tractors because of their small size.

Three more tractors from Yanmar rounded out the line by 1984. The 1250 used a three-cylinder naturally-aspirated diesel, the 1450 used a four-cylinder naturally aspirated engine, and the 1650 used the same four-cylinder engine with a turbocharger. The Model 1250 was rated at 41 PTO horsepower, 51 PTO horsepower for the 1450, and 62 PTO horsepower for the 1650.

A 2030 tractor is shown in this late 1972 photo sporting a Roll-Gard roll over protection system (ROPS). The mower is a No. 350 three-point type, V-belt driven.

Engine improvements in the four Mannheim tractors for 1983 resulted in a five-horsepower increase for each model. Improved hydraulics allowed faster lifting of heavy loads and better connections of remote cylinders. All but the Model 2150 could be ordered with the Sound-Gard cab. The Model 2150 was rated at 46 PTO horsepower, the 2350 at 56 PTO horsepower, the 2550 at 66 PTO horsepower, and the 2750 at 75 PTO horsepower.

The Model 2950 was introduced in 1983. This Mannheim-built tractor used a 359ci six-cylinder engine, up from the 329ci of the previous model. It featured twelve forward speeds, including those provided by the partial-range power shift. The tractor was rated at 85 PTO horsepower and had a basic weight of about 10,000lb.

Five of the Waterloo favorites were improved for 1983. The 4250 and 4450 were offered in the Hi-Crop configuration. The 4050 had the naturally-aspirated 404ci engine of 101 PTO horsepower, and the rest used the 466ci engine with the following variations: the 4240 was naturally aspirated and was rated at 123hp; the 4440 was turbocharged for 140hp; the 4640,

165hp from the turbocharged and intercooled engine. The new 4840 used the same engine, but increased turbocharger boost gave it 193hp.

Engine improvements in the four 55 Series Mannheim tractors resulted in improved fuel economy in 1987. The Model 2155, with the three-cylinder 179ci engine, was rated at 45 PTO horsepower. The 2350 had a four-cylinder engine of 239ci rated at 55hp. The 2550 used the same size four-cylinder engine as the 2355, but it was turbocharged and yielded 65hp. The 2755 at 75hp, also used this four-cylinder engine, but with increased turbo boost. A variation of the 2755 was the Model 2855N (for narrow), an orchard tractor rated at 80hp.

The Model 2955, introduced in 1987 to replace the 2950, used a 359ci six-cylinder engine rated at 86hp. It featured twelve forward speeds, including those provided by the partial-range power shift. The tractor had a basic weight of about 10,000lb.

The End of the Era

In 1975, William Hewitt, with an eye toward orderly management succession, created the

Mexico, 1974; a big turbocharged Model 4435 plows with a No. 3751 disk plow. The 4435 was a Monterey, Mexico, built 125hp machine. The Mexican-built 35 Series tractors were unveiled in 1973 with the 4435 and 4235. The Model 2535 and 2735 came out in 1975. These four stayed in the lineup until 1983, when they were replaced by the Mexican-built 55 Series.

John Deere took another flyer in the bicycle business in 1974. The Commercial Products Division imported ten, five, and three-speed bikes for a time and handled some single-speed 20in kids bikes.

A Model 4630 tractor pulls a No. 350 Level-Action (double off-set) disk in this 1975 photo. The disk was called a double off-set because the gangs overlapped to eliminate the center rut. The 4630 was a 150hp Waterloo tractor.

post of executive vice president and appointed Robert A. Hanson to fill it. It was not a foregone conclusion that Hanson would succeed Hewitt, but everyone knew that was what was intended.

Hanson had come up through the ranks, spending many years in the foreign operations. His selection pointed out the importance of appreciating the worldwide scope of Deere & Company.

Robert A. Hanson was given the title of president, chairman, and chief executive officer in 1982. William Hewitt retired at the mandatory age of 67, which he himself had established. Ended was an unbroken 145 year history of family leadership.

The company is now past 158 years old. That makes it one of the oldest. But Deere is unique in another way. There is what is known as the Deere "attitude." It's an attitude that borders on the nostalgic. From the mahogany offices to the production floor, there is a universal respect for the past. Deere men and women believe in their company, not so much because it's their company, but because they feel the company deserves it! This respect for the past is reflected in their concern for the future; in maintaining the traditional qualities of product and service. Any shortcoming in the way each employee does his or her daily job is like a breach of trust—a failure to live up to the tradition.

Even though Deere & Company is no longer managed by a Deere family member, there has been a succession of able chief executives who have carried on the traditions. The company's reputation for well-engineered products and superb service is as high as ever.

John Deere made both three-point and drawn-type mowers in 1975. Shown here is a No. 450 drawn mower with a 2630 tractor. The 2630 was a 70hp tractor built in both Mannheim and Dubuque.

The Model 3130 was one of John Deere's "World Wide tractors." It was built in both Germany and Spain. It is shown here in 1978, with a No. 148 farm loader.

A big 8640 four-wheel drive is shown with a 7000 Series sixteen-row front-folding planter. The 8640 boasted a 619ci turbocharged and intercooled diesel of 229hp. The 8640 was built in model years 1979 through 1982.

In 1975, utility tractors were designated as the 40 Series. They were given Generation II styling. Roll-Gard structures were standard. The 2240 was a 50hp tractor. The orchard version is shown here with a mounted sprayer. These were Mannheim-built tractors.

John Deere began in the plow business and has maintained a presence in that business, although plowing is not done routinely anymore. These 1979 model gang plows have safety trips and spring resets. The 2600 plow is on the left (four to six bottoms); the 2800 plow is on the right (four to eight bottoms). *Deere Archives*

The Fifty Series tractors were announced in 1982. Utility tractors, like this Model 2750, were made in Mannheim, while industrial versions were made in Dubuque. The 2750 had a four-cylinder turbocharged engine of 75hp. It is shown in this 1982 photo pulling an 8000 Series end-wheel drill.

The Model 1650 was a turbocharged 62hp Yanmar-built fifty Series tractor. At the time of its Nebraska test, the 1650 was the most fuel efficient tractor ever tested. This 1650 is shown in 1983 with a No. 100 farm loader and a rear blade.

The Yanmar-built 1650, 62hp tractor was available in an orchard configuration and with front-wheel drive, as shown here. The 1650 was built in year models 1984 through 1987.

The JD860-A was the leading sixteen-yard scraper in the late 1960s. Deere pioneered the "elevating" scraper, with conveyor-like paddles that carry the dirt back and up, when they became allied with the Hancock Scraper Company in 1952. Elevating scrapers fill with less horsepower. The elevator also tends to pulverize the dirt, making it easier to spread when unloading.

By 1965, the variety of three; four; and six-cylinder diesel engines in Deere's stable led to a number of new applications. The Industrial Equipment Division, established in 1956, moved into the logging industry in a big way. Three new log skidders were introduced that year: the JD440, the JD540, and the big JD740 shown in this photo. Experience with the articulated Model 8020 tractor was applied to these skidders; they could bend in the middle up to 45 degrees for steering. Each was equipped with an arch and a cable drum in the rear. The operator could pull out the cable with several smaller choker cables. The chokers would be wrapped around the butts of as many as seven logs. The winch would then pull them all in and raise the butts beneath the arch. The machine can then pull the logs, with the small ends dragging, across virtually any terrain, to a landing site where they can be loaded onto trucks for hauling to the mill. The blade in front is used for decking the logs at the landing, for rooting out stumps and humps that would snag the skidder from underneath, and for leveling and snowplowing for the hauling trucks. In the 1970s and 1980s, skidders with hydraulic grapples overtook the cable skidders in popularity. Skidders were powered with engines from 90hp to 135hp. Deere also went into the manufacture of wheeled and tracked feller bunchers. These machines cut standing trees, lay them down, cut the limbs off, cut the trunks to length, and then stack them for a hauling skidder

JOHN DEERE INTRODUCES NEW 8000 SERIES TRACTORS

Now get UNPRECEDENTED visibility, maneuverability, power, and control

John Deere introduces 21st Century Technology Today. The revolutionary new CommandARM puts engine, transmission, hitch, hydraulics, and PTO in the palm of your hand. And high-torque 7.6 and new 8.1 L engines, with exclusive electronic engine control, deliver near constant-torque performance to as low 1,000 rpm. Teamed with our all-new, ultra-efficient 16-speed Power Shift transmission, you get more power to the ground. Plus, speeds in the working range progress in productive 1/2-mph increments to let you match conditions perfectly. And new 8000 Series Tractors feature high-pressure, high-capacity hydraulics, with over 15,000 pound hitch lift capacity (optional on the two largest models) to add greatly to your abilities.

PATENTED TRACTOR DESIGN *We moved the engine forward 44 inches, and raised it 10, to create a tractor configuration that not only opens your view to both front wheels, but also provides the tightest, narrow-row MFWD turn radius in the industry.*

NOW: ALL MAJOR TRACTOR FUNCTIONS ARE IN THE PALM OF YOUR HAND
Even if you swivel your seat the full 20 degrees right, or 15 degrees left, the CommandARM moves with you...so everything is at your fingertips. Nobody else has anything like it.

JOHN DEERE

A farm magazine ad from 1994 introduces John Deere's new 8000 series tractors. Note the weight rack on the front of he 160hp model 8100 tractor.

The 4400 combine was a four-walker, 95hp machine, shown here with a two-row corn head. It was similar in design to the 3300, except the 3300 used only three walkers. These two, plus the four-walker 6600 and the 5-walker 7700 represented the New Generation combines of introduced in 1968.

Another 4400 combine, this one with a grain head and a factory air conditioned cab.

The John Deere 4020 was one of the greatest tractors of all times. It was introduced with the Twenty Series in the fall of 1963. The 4020's six-cylinder engine was available in gasoline, LPG, and diesel versions, all of which produced a rated 95 PTO horsepower. The displacement of the gasoline and LPG engines was 340ci, while the diesel was 404ci. The 4020, like its stable-mate the 3020, was built at the Waterloo Tractor Works. It weighed about 8,900lb. *Deere Archives*

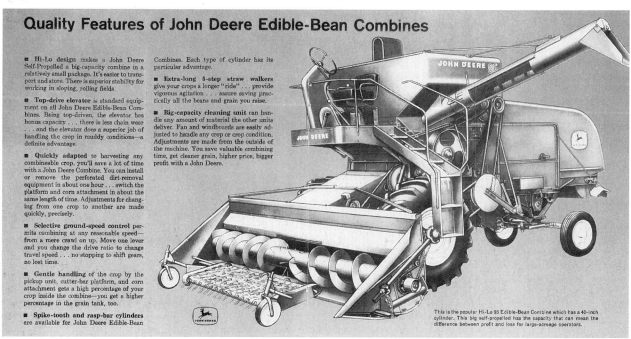

Ad copy for the John Deere Edible-Bean Combine is shown in this 1965 picture. Edible bean combines had special stone and dirt traps and sensors.

The John Deere Industrial Equipment Division brought out the JD 570 motor grader in 1967. It was the first of a line of motor graders that now includes six sizes from 90hp to 200hp. The original JD 570 was rated at 83hp. The JD 570-A, shown here, was brought out in 1972.

Deere's motor grader concept pioneered the articulated frame. The grader could bend in the middle for sharper turns and for stability on hillsides. Hydrostatic front wheel assist was a popular option.

The Model 5020 was built between 1966 and 1972. It was the successor to the Model 5010, which was the first two-wheel drive tractor to break the 100hp barrier. The 5020 was rated at 133hp (141hp on a later test with the power shift transmission). The six-cylinder engine was available as a diesel only. It displaced 531ci. The 5020 was offered in standard tread and row-crop versions. Its normal weight was about 16,000 pounds, but with ballast weights of over 21,000lb were not uncommon. *Deere Archives*

Below—**New 105 Corn Special** with 812 Attachment for harvesting eight 20-inch rows. Engines on John Deere 105 Combines have been boosted to 105 horsepower for 1968, and an electric fuel pump guards against vapor lock. All Corn Specials have the extra-heavy, extra-husky construction needed for harvesting corn.

Above—**New 55 Corn Special** with 335 Attachment, adjustable for 30-, 36-, 38-, or 40-inch rows. Notice the large "basket" area, the long, low gatherers, and shields on the center points which can be removed for harvesting down corn. All John Deere Combines have extra-strong 22-inch-diameter cylinders, 30 inches wide on the 55, 40 on the 95, and 50 on the big 105.

Ad copy from the year 1968 for Corn Special combines. The 55 was introduced in 1946, but was continuously upgraded over the years. The 95 combine was introduced in 1958, with the big 105 following in 1961. These combines originally used four-speed transmissions with variable-speed V-belt drives. By 1968, when this ad appeared, hydrostatic transmissions were an increasingly accepted option.

The Thirty Series tractors were introduced in 1972. The 5020 was replaced by the 6030, shown here. The 6030 used a turbocharged and intercooled six-cylinder engine of 175hp. In 1973, the 6030 was offered with the non-turbocharged 5020 engine, which offered 141hp. *Deere Archives*

John Deere gained a reputation for crawler tractors when the Lindeman Brothers of Yakima, Washington, added tracks to the venerable Model BO tractor. By 1965, a complete line of modern crawler-dozers was available. Shown here is a 65hp Model JD 450-B, which was introduced in 1970.

The 6600 New Generation combine was introduced in 1968, but the Hillside version was added in 1975. The Hillside 6600 utilized paddle conveyors which helped prevent cleaning losses when the header was tilted.

A 1995 ad for the Model 9965 cotton picker. This harvester can pick seven acres in an hour.

Pull-type PTO combines cut the cost of owning a harvester for many a farmer. Utilizing the increasing tractor horsepower made these big machines practical and economical. Shown here is a 4430 tractor, with Sound-Gard Body, pulling and powering a 6601 combine. The 4430 was a Waterloo tractor of 126 PTO horsepower. The 6601 was a U.S. made four-walker combine with a 100 bushel tank and 13ft platform. This photo was taken in September of 1973.

The dual-path hydrostatic drive made this 110hp JD 755 crawler-loader extremely maneuverable and productive. It was introduced in 1976.

The 4400 combine was popular in the Midwest in the 1970s. It is shown here with a Forty Series four-row corn head. *Deere Archives*

The 40 Series John Deere Waterloo-built tractors were introduced in 1975. The most popular was the 4440, shown here with a 1508 rotary cutter. The 4440 used the 466ci naturally aspirated 6-cylinder diesel engine, rated at 130 PTO horsepower. *Deere Archives*

The Model 4050 John Deere tractor replaced the venerable 4040 in 1983. It used a six-cylinder 466ci engine, naturally aspirated, of 101hp. It is shown here with a Sound-Gard cab and a 250 sprayer. *Deere Archives*

This 1978 version of the pull-type combine is a Model 7721. It was the equivalent of the 7720 self-propelled combine. Although no head is installed for the photo, this machine accommodates 12ft to 14ft platforms.

The Turbo 7700, shown in this 1978 photo has hydrostatic drive and a 218 grain platform. New Generation combines were upgraded in 1974 with a rotating engine cooling screen (the cylinder protruding above the right front tire). A vacuum arm removed chaff and trash that accumulated on the screen. New Generation combines featured Deere's patented Quik-Tatch system, which allowed switching between platforms and corn-heads.

Titan combines were introduced in 1979. The 7720 Titan II, shown here in the rice, replaced the 7720 Titan in 1985. Dual front wheels and hydrostatically-driven rear steering wheels were a welcome option for rice operations.

Compact tractors were brought out by the Consumer Products Division in 1978. Made by Yanmar in Japan, the new compacts had small, efficient diesel engines. The first models introduced were the 22hp 850 and the 27hp 950. The 33hp Model 1050, shown here, came out in 1980.

Yanmar-built Consumer Products tractors were all-gear drive. The compact 650, a 14.5hp machine was the small-est Yanmar-Deere. The 650 was added to the line in 1980.

The compact Model 650 Yanmar-built was designed for use with a 60in rotary mower deck. A diesel engine, me-chanical front-wheel drive and a Category 1 three-point hitch gave the 650 big tractor features.

The Model 2750 replaced the 2640 in 1983. It was built through the 1986 model year. The 75hp tractor is shown here with a 260 mower. *Deere Archives*

The Yanmar-built Model 750 compact tractor came out with an 18hp diesel in 1981. Although designed for farm use, most found their way to estates and golf courses with either belly, or three-point mowers.

This ad from 1995 shows how to cut a quarter acre more per hour with Deere 710 and 720 mowers.

The 4250 tractor with a 327 baler is shown in this 1986 photo taken near Cedar Falls, Iowa. The 4250 was introduced in 1984. It was a Waterloo-built six-cylinder turbocharged tractor with 120 PTO horsepower.

Horicon-built compact tractors introduced in 1986 were the models 655, 755, and 855. Engines were three-cylinder diesels by Yanmar of Japan. Sundstrand two-range hydrostatic drives were featured. The 655 shown here is equipped with a Category 1 three-point hitch.

Hydrostatic drive made the compact diesel-powered 855 tractor a great mowing machine. Mechanical front-wheel drive and power steering were options. The 855 was brought out in 1986

The Yanmar-Deere Model 2255 was like the 2155, except it was available in orchard and vineyard configuration. The 2255 was a three-cylinder diesel machine of 50hp. The orchard model was about 6in wider than the vineyard model. Orchard/vineyard tractors were the only John Deere tractors (except for lawn tractors) after 1984 not to be equipped with roll-bar protection.

The Consumer Products Division produced this Model 655 tractor with a 60in mower deck and a hydraulic grass-catcher dump. The 655 was introduced in 1986. It used a three-cylinder Yanmar diesel engine and a two-range Sundstrand hydrostatic transmission. Power steering was standard. *Deere Archives*

The Industrial Model 2555 tractors, like the farm versions, were built in both Dubuque and Mannheim. They were 65hp four-cylinder machines. Dealers were selling the 2555 for about $23,000 in 1987.

"For a tractor this size, I am impressed with its power and fuel efficiency."

J.L. Watring uses his John Deere 5400 Tractor for just about everything on his growing row-crop and livestock farm in Blackwater, Missouri.

"My 5400 is rated at 60 hp, but it works like it has 80 or 85," says J.L. "The first thing I did was cultivate with a 6-row cultivator. A 6-row cultivator is a pretty good load for a tractor this size, but with the MFWD (mechanical front-wheel drive), the tractor just played with it."

Speaking of MFWD, J.L. declares, "It amazed me how the MFWD would turn with the wheels set in on 30-inch rows. You can turn around on a dime."

And J.L. loves the fuel efficiency. "As hard as I've ever pulled the engine down, the tractor has only used about a gallon and a half of fuel per hour."

This hydraulic pump provides up to 2,750 psi to break-out heavy loads. And you get the highest total standard flow rate (18.2 gpm) in this horsepower class, for super-quick cycle times.

J.L.'s 5400 provides ample hydraulic power, too. "This tractor has tons of hydraulic power. The hydraulic pump on our hay rake runs continuously. On 100-degree days, you can run the rake all day and the system doesn't get hot, and you still have all the power you need."

See a 40-hp 5200, 50-hp 5300, or 60-hp 5400 today at your John Deere dealer's. J.L. says you won't be disappointed. "I've run every tractor made in this size. I decided I needed to buy a John Deere. I am well satisfied."

J.L. Watring: *Blackwater, Missouri*   Off-farm occupation: *Owns milk route*
Farm operation: *Cattle, hogs, corn, beans*   Tractor: *John Deere 5400 with 540 Loader*

A contemporary ad for John Deere.

Mechanical front-wheel drive was standard on the Horicon, Wisconsin-built 955 compact diesel tractor. The tall foot pedal on the right side of the tractor is for the brakes; the other two shorter pedals control the Sundstrand hydrostatic transmission. Roll-Gard ROPS and a seat belt were standard equipment on the 955, which was introduced in 1989.

John Deere broke new ground with their AMT series of utility vehicles. Shown here is the AMT 600 of 1987. AMT stood for All-Material-Transport. Single-cylinder engines by Kawasaki were used, along with variable-ratio V-belt drives. These vehicles were made in Deere's Welland Works in Ontario, Canada.

The 1158 was a European combine introduced in 1989. It featured a 24x41in cylinder and a 127hp engine. *Deere Archives*

John Deere has carved out a niche for itself in the bulldozer field since the MC crawler dozer of 1947. Shown here is a 1990 Model 400G; a 60hp favorite of construction contractors. *Deere Archives*

The 235 PTO horsepower 8650 four-wheel drive was in- transmission with sixteen speeds. It's pulling a 716A for-
troduced in 1982. It featured a single-lever Quad-Range age wagon. *Deere Archives*

The 870 was a Yanmar-built 18.5hp three-cylinder diesel
engine. Big tractor features were disk brakes and live
PTO.

The Model 70 mini-excavator features a tracked undercarriage and a dozer blade for backfilling. It was popular in the European market. *Deere Archives*

Index